companion
PIECES

Carolyn Sullivan

D1567442

A J.B. Fairfax Press Publication

THE QUILTER'S WORKSHOP

EDITORIAL
MANAGING EDITOR
Judy Poulos
EDITORIAL ASSISTANT
Ella Martin

PHOTOGRAPHY
Andrew Payne
Andre Martin
STYLING
Anne-Maree Unwin

PRODUCTION AND DESIGN
PRODUCTION DIRECTOR
Anna Maguire
PRODUCTION COORDINATOR
Meredith Johnston
PRODUCTION ASSISTANT
Heather Straton
DESIGN MANAGER
Drew Buckmaster
LAYOUT
Lulu Dougherty
COVER DESIGN
Sheridan Packer

PUBLISHED BY J.B. Fairfax Press Pty Limited
80-82 McLachlan Ave
Rushcutters Bay
Australia NSW 2011
A.C.N. 003 738 430

WEB ADDRESS: http://www.jbfp.com.au

FORMATTED BY J.B. Fairfax Press Pty Limited

PRINTED BY Toppan Printing Co. Singapore
© J.B. Fairfax Press Pty Limited 1998

JBFP 503

COMPANION PIECES
ISBN 1 86343 329 5

DISTRIBUTION & SALES
Australia: J.B. Fairfax Press Pty Limited
Ph: (02) 9361 6366; Fax: (02) 9360 6262
USA: Quilters' Resource Inc.
2211 Nth Elston Ave, Chicago 60614
Ph: (773) 278 5695; Fax: (773) 278 1348

Contents

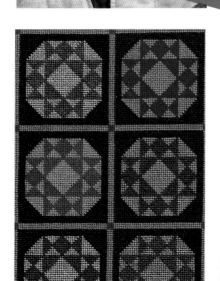

About the author

I have always been fascinated with what the world looks like. After completing an Arts degree, where I majored in geography, I spent many years teaching in secondary schools, sharing this love with a not always appreciative audience. I have travelled quite extensively, particularly in Asia and the United States, and always enjoyed sharing my experiences with my students.

Travelling in Australia is equally exciting. Recent trips to Lake Mungo National Park in far western New South Wales and to Tasmania, have instilled in me an awe of the landscape.

I read many books and collect pictures, which I save into scrapbooks. These have become very important in my life, almost an end in themselves, as they allow me to keep a reference of all the things I have seen, read about or visited. As I learn more and more about design, the scrapbooks are becoming a reference of the ideas I have designed, as well as the ideas of others, and places seen. I am excited by all of these and they are always at the back of my mind as I sew.

During my recent term as president of The Quilters' Guild in New South Wales, I had the opportunity to participate in many exciting quilting events and to meet the friendly and talented people who are part of the quilting and embroidery world.

Since then, I have rejoined the embroidery groups, which are very important to me, providing the opportunities for more learning and friendship with like-minded stitchers.

Acknowledgments

One of the benefits of a close, extended family is that every member is supported in all that they wish to do, and all members are involved to one extent or another. This has been the case for me. I want to thank them all, particularly my husband, Ken, whose continuing encouragement and love have been essential.

My thanks to Karen Fail and Judy Poulos at J.B. Fairfax Press for their support and advice; and to Lynn Hewitt, a good friend and proofreader.

My thanks also to Theo Stamatopoulos of Gold Leaf Framing, Como West, for wanting the embroideries to look their best and making sure that they do.

The generous support of DMC (Australia) Pty Ltd is also appreciated.

Introduction

I love quilts! I also love embroidery! Stitchery has been part of my life since I was in my teens, but I have always had textiles around me. My grandmother crocheted fine articles for her family and for the church. My mother, sister and daughter always have textile-related projects on the go. This family tradition supports the all-consuming role quilts and embroidery play in my life.

One of my earliest attempts at embroidery (other than basic skills taught at school) was a piece of painted tapestry canvas of some rather lurid fish. Good taste was not the intent. Learning the technique and having fun were more important. I continue to love canvas embroidery, particularly where colour is the dominant feature. Although I have learned many embroidery techniques over the years, I still love playing with colours and patterns.

Like all quiltmakers, I love the variety of patterns that can be made into wonderful textiles for our homes and families. Playing with the fabrics is part of the fun. Making 'companion pieces' – a quilt with matching embroidery – seemed a way to stitch some of my favourite quilt patterns as well as to create some new ones.

All of the quilts in this book are based on simple blocks, both traditional and new. The traditional designs that I have used, allow for many variations. The Ohio Star pattern is one of my favourites. Its many variations can be as simple or as complex as you want them to be.

Inspiration comes from the most unlikely sources! For a number of years I observed the way the shadows fell in the hallway of my house when certain lights were on. I actually sat down one night and sketched the patterns. Shortly afterwards it occurred to me that these drawings could be simplified, then rotated. Perhaps I reinvented the wheel! The number of quilts that can be made by rotating a simple design is endless – the only limitation being the time in which to explore the options. Lots of dynamic quilts can be produced this way.

Enjoy the projects! I have certainly enjoyed making them. However, I would be equally pleased to see you create your own designs using the ideas and techniques outlined here. I have also enjoyed playing with all the colours. However, these are my colour choices; you can find much pleasure in selecting your own.

Above all – have fun!

Carolyn

Patchwork Techniques

There are many methods of quiltmaking – each has its own advantage. When working with very small pieces, foundation piecing provides great accuracy, as does English paper-piecing. For me, there are times when any kind of hand-piecing is relaxing. I choose my method for the result I want to achieve and how fast I want to finish. While the majority of quilts in this book are made by machine, using quick-cutting methods, there is an English hand-pieced quilt and there are two quilts made with foundation-piecing.

CUTTING AND PIECING
Preparing the fabric

Prewashing fabric is important to remove the chemicals which are used to finish the fabrics and ensure they are colourfast.

Much quick piecing relies on cutting strips of fabric from selvage to selvage. The selvages must be folded edge to edge. This can often mean that the raw edges will not be matching.

To correct this, fold the fabric widthwise, then place the folded edge exactly along the selvages. Place your ruler so that one of the cross lines on the ruler lines up with the fold of the fabric. Make a neat cut, trimming away the excess fabric (Fig. 1). This may seem wasteful, but it will ensure that all the strips are cut straight.

Now, turn your cutting board through an angle of 180 degrees, without disturbing the fabric, so the straight cut edge is now on the left-hand side. Commence cutting the strips from the left-hand side.

Rotary-cutting techniques

Accurate measuring and rotary cutting is essential to ensure your quilt comes together properly. One set of measurements that I employ is the relationship between a square, a half-square triangle and a quarter-square triangle (Fig. 2). This measurement technique ensures a 7.5 mm ($\frac{1}{4}$ in) seam allowance and accurate piecing.

For cutting squares, the general rule is to add 1.5 cm ($\frac{1}{2}$ in) (Fig. 3). If a finished piece is to be 8 cm ($3\frac{1}{4}$ in) square, add 1.5 cm ($\frac{1}{2}$ in) to each side. Cut the strip 9.5 cm ($3\frac{3}{4}$ in) wide, then cut the strip into 9.5 cm ($3\frac{3}{4}$ in) squares.

For cutting half-square triangles, the general rule is to add 2.5 cm ($\frac{7}{8}$ in) (Fig. 4). If a finished half-square triangle is needed to match the 8 cm ($3\frac{1}{4}$ in) square, add 2.5 cm ($\frac{7}{8}$ in), so the strip is cut 10.5 cm ($4\frac{1}{8}$ in) wide, then cut it into 10.5 cm ($4\frac{1}{8}$ in) squares. Cut each square across one diagonal only.

For quarter-square triangles, the general rule is to add 3.5 cm ($1\frac{1}{4}$ in) (Fig. 5). If a finished quarter-square triangle is needed to match the square and half-square triangle described above, add 3.5 cm ($1\frac{1}{4}$ in), so the strip is cut 11.5 cm ($4\frac{1}{2}$ in) wide, then cut into 11.5 cm ($4\frac{1}{2}$ in) squares, then cut across both diagonals.

Piecing

Accurate piecing is very important and can be achieved by following a few simple hints.

When two seams are to be matched, it is much easier if the seam allowances are pressed in opposite directions (Fig. 6). I have called this 'butting seams' and have referred to this often in the pressing instructions.

Another method I use for more complex joins is the 'three-pin' method: With the right sides together, place the two pieces together. Put a pin through the two points you wish to meet. Keeping this pin upright, place a pin very close on either side of it at right angles to the seam line, pinning through all thicknesses. Remove the upright pin and stitch the seam.

Chain-piecing

When there are many pieces to be joined that are basically the same, it is best to keep feeding them through the machine without stopping at the end of each pair, cutting the thread and starting again (Fig. 7). This saves thread and much time!

Hand-piecing

There are two types of hand-piecing in patchwork. The first, generally called American piecing, is where paper or plastic templates are accurately drawn to the finished sizes of the pieces. They are used to mark the stitching lines on the back of the fabric. When the pieces are cut out, an additional 7.5 mm (¼ in) is added for the seam allowance. The pieces are stitched together in a sequential manner, right sides facing, stitching on the marked lines and accurately matching the points.

The other method is called English piecing and was used for 'Watercolour' on page 29. Here, metal templates are used to cut paper cards which are the finished sizes of the pieces. Fabric shapes are cut, adding the 7.5 mm (¼ in) seam allowance as before.

The three-pin method

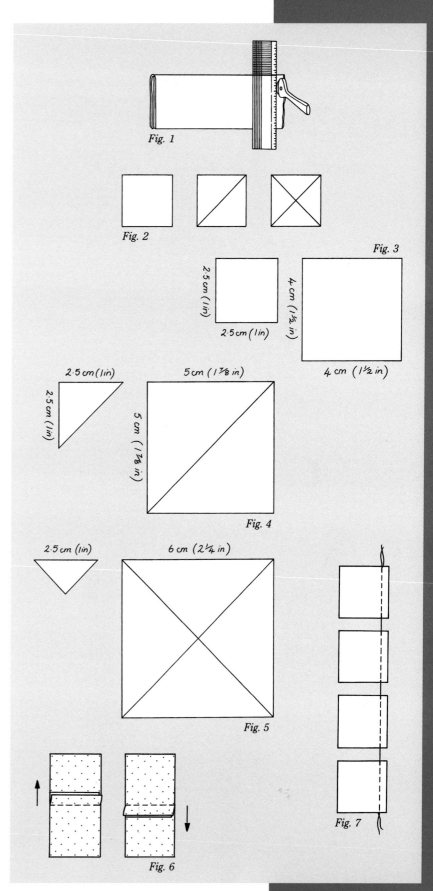

Fig. 1

Fig. 2

Fig. 3

2·5 cm (1in)

2·5 cm (1in)

4 cm (1½ in)

4 cm (1½ in)

2·5 cm (1in)

2·5 cm (1in)

5 cm (1⅞ in)

5 cm (1⅞ in)

Fig. 4

2·5 cm (1in)

6 cm (2¼ in)

Fig. 5

Fig. 6

Fig. 7

The fabric shape is then basted over the card. Adjacent fabric-covered cards are joined with an oversewing stitch, to form the block. The papers are then removed. While this method is very time-consuming, it ensures great accuracy, especially when working with very small pieces.

Foundation-piecing

This method has become popular in recent times as it allows for very accurate machine-piecing of small shapes. Here, the pieces of fabric are stitched onto a foundation of paper, calico or interfacing. The stitching lines are drawn in reverse, onto the back of the foundation. I like to use a fine, non-iron, non-woven interfacing. Small pieces of fabric are stitched onto the foundation along the drawn lines, working from the back.

Some foundations are removed or torn away. Because I use interfacing, mine are left in place and provide a lovely base for work.

Borders

I always find borders the fun part of the quilt. However, they are very important as they give the quilt a finished look.

There are many different styles of borders – two or three different widths as in 'Floriade Pansies' on page 45; pieced; an exciting fabric which is a feature in itself; with a plain block corner, as in 'A Blaze of Stars' on page 13; with a pieced block corner, as in 'Central Space' on page 34. The choices are almost limitless.

To determine the length of the borders, measure the quilt across the centre and cut the first borders to this length. The second borders are cut to this length plus the width of the first two borders, or cut to the actual size if corner squares are to be added.

When attaching the borders, always match the centre of the border to the centre of the side, then pin out to the edges.

Most commonly, I add the top and

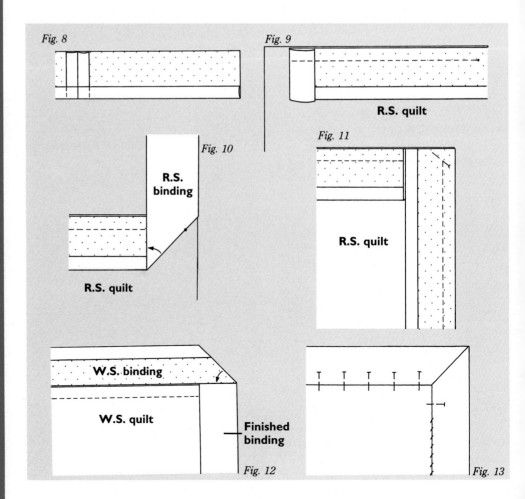

Fig. 8

Fig. 9

R.S. quilt

Fig. 10

R.S. binding

R.S. quilt

Fig. 11

R.S. quilt

W.S. binding

W.S. quilt

Finished binding

Fig. 12

Fig. 13

bottom borders first and press the seam towards the border, then I attach the side borders and press in the same way.

Occasionally, I will mitre the corners of the borders and stitch this seam by hand. I have used this method for 'Watercolour' on page 29 and 'Red Sails' on page 69.

Bindings

To make the bindings for straight-edge quilts, I cut lengths of fabric from selvage to selvage, 3–4 cm (1¼–1½ in) wide, and join them to make one long strip. You will need to work out how many of these strips to cut for each quilt.

I then press in 7.5 mm (¼ in) on one long edge of the binding strip (Fig. 8). Pin the raw edge of the binding to the edge of the right side of the quilt, starting at a suitable point. For me this is not a corner, as I like to line up with a seam that is already on the quilt. Before you begin stitching, turn under a small hem on the end of the binding so that when the binding is stitched and turned to the back of the quilt, the raw end is hidden. Pin the binding along the entire edge, stretching it very slightly as you go. Put the first pin in so that the next seam is exactly the same width as the one you have just pinned. Stitch along the binding, stopping at the last pin. Do a small back stitch, then cut off the threads (Fig. 9).

Fold the binding back at an angle of 45 degrees (Fig. 10), then fold it again so the raw edge lies along the next side of the quilt to be bound (Fig. 11). Place the first pin in the last stitch you did on the previous row and pin along the edge as before. Begin stitching at the first pin. Complete all sides of the quilt in the same way.

When the binding is attached to all four sides, turn the quilt over and turn all the binding over onto the back of the quilt, covering the raw edges. Make sure that the binding is 'filled' and there is no empty space inside it. At the corners, lay one edge flat, so that an angle of 45 degrees is formed by the binding (Fig. 12). Fold the new edge over the first and pin, then hem by hand (Fig. 13).

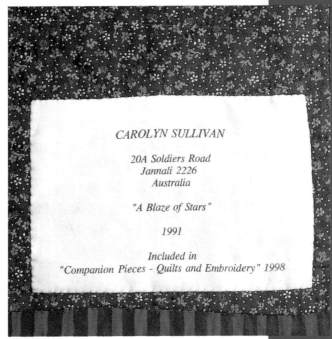

CAROLYN SULLIVAN

20A Soldiers Road
Jannali 2226
Australia

"A Blaze of Stars"

1991

Included in
"Companion Pieces - Quilts and Embroidery" 1998

**The label from
'A Blaze of Stars'**

Labels

So much is written about the importance of labels and it cannot be underestimated. The label should include your name, address, quilt completion date and the name of the quilt. What a fantastic body of documented art work will be left for future generations!

EQUIPMENT AND MATERIALS

- A well-maintained sewing machine is essential, as is a sharp needle – don't wait for the needle to break before changing it.
- A rotary cutter, ruler and self-healing cutting mat assists most patchwork.
- While I generally use one hundred per cent cotton fabric because it is so lovely to work with, there are times when any fabric will do, if it suits the purpose and you can manage it, as some fabrics are very slippery and fray.
- When selecting a thread, the usual rule is to use a colour that matches the darker of the pieces being joined. However, with fast piecing it is sometimes better to select a neutral thread, such as grey, bone, black, white or navy. Sometimes, more than one colour of thread is needed in the making of a quilt, if the thread is not to show.

COLOUR SELECTION

A lot has been written about colour. One of the pleasures – and agonies – of making these quilts has been choosing the colours. I do not have particular artistic qualifications, but I do enjoy collecting photographs whose colours excite me. This collection is always available for reference. I also cut pictures from magazines and put them in a scrapbook. One picture which has stimulated many colour decisions is of burgundy and fawn birds against the background of a mound of mud. The touches of turquoise on the tail feathers were very eye-catching, and the combination of drab colours with this vibrant highlight produced some very exciting quilts and embroideries.

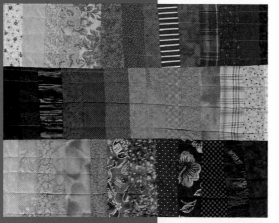

A colour sampler

I also borrow books on all sorts of topics from my local library – travel, art, nature, costumes, fabrics, photography, jewellery, architecture and home design (particularly from other cultures). Of course, these pictures can't be cut out, but you can copy them with paints or coloured pencils.

When I can, I visit art galleries, particularly the special exhibitions. I took my DMC chart to the 'Fauves' exhibition at the Art Gallery of New South Wales, and wrote thread numbers all over my catalogue as I matched the threads to the colours in the paintings. I will never slavishly reproduce the paintings, but the colour combinations are there for reference.

Photocopy a range of colours to find light and dark

I also take my own photographs. My camera is a single lens reflex camera with a good close-up facility.

None of this confidence with colour has come quickly – it is only through the accumulation of ideas over time. I am aware, however, that informed colour decisions can rely on knowing two valuable pieces of information.

Being able to distinguish between warm and cool colours is important. I always think of the warm colours as those you can see in the sunset – yellow, gold, orange, red, mauve, purple and burgundy. They give an impression of warmth. Cool colours are those I associate with water – blue, green, turquoise etc – and are very refreshing.

You may make a colour choice that is mostly warm as in 'Follow the Shades' on page 75. Its small touches of cool colour are a highlight. Or, you may prefer cool colours as in 'Blue Medallion' on page 23. In this piece, the golds highlight the blues. 'Lovable Linda' on page 18 and 'Central Space' on page 34 use cool and warm colours equally and are effective in their own ways. All are acceptable – finding the balance is important.

Knowing about the value of your colour choice is also important. You need to be able to distinguish between light, medium and dark values. This is what will provide contrast in your work. The English-pieced 'Watercolour' on page 29 relies entirely on the contrast between light and dark fabrics to achieve its effect. 'Central Space' on page 34 also relies on this contrast.

Most often, your eye will tell you if the fabrics you have chosen are light, medium or dark. If you have a large range of fabrics and wish to range them from light to dark, it is best to paste small pieces of them on to a piece of paper and photocopy them. This will give you instant feedback and allow you to make whatever changes you wish.

Embroidery Techniques

The embroidery I have used in this book is known as canvas work or needlepoint. It is worked on a fine, heavily starched cloth with easily seen, equally spaced threads.

EQUIPMENT AND MATERIALS

Canvas All of the embroideries have been worked on Zweigart No. 9406.127.194 Congress cloth, which has a 24 count. This means that there are twenty-five threads to the inch or ten threads to one centimetre. When cutting a piece of canvas ready for work, it is best to allow 4–5 cm (1½–2 in) extra all around what you expect will be the finished work. This gives you some leeway, as well as having extra fabric to assist with the framing, when it is completed.

Threads All of the work is done with three strands of DMC Stranded Cotton.

Frames I have always worked on a frame as this helps to give an even tension to the piece and keeps it in shape. There are many different types of frames available – it is a matter of finding one that you are comfortable working with.

Pencil Mark the centre point on the canvas with a pencil before mounting onto the frame.

Needles For fine canvas like this, it is best to use a good quality no. 26 tapestry needle. Tapestry needles are blunt and allow the needle to pass through the holes of the canvas easily, without splitting the threads.

STITCHING

Even tension when stitching is very important for a pleasing result. Tension refers to how tight or loose the work is. If the work is too tight, the canvas will show through. If it is too loose, the threads will loop and catch. If you are unsure of your tension, it is always advisable to practise on a small area in the border of your canvas before you begin.

Use a short thread, about 30–35 cm (12–14 in). Longer threads can become quite frayed from being continuously pulled through the strong canvas. Sometimes, I snip off the frayed end of the thread as I work, to avoid fluffing.

While there are a number of stitches that can be used for this work, I prefer to use basketweave stitch as it gives a good coverage of the canvas. For this stitch, bring the needle up through the canvas at the odd numbers and take it down through the canvas at the even numbers (Fig. 1).

Above: Detail of embroidery
Below: Assorted frames and threads

READING THE CHARTS

A chart is provided for each of the embroideries in the book. Some people are daunted by charts, but there is no need to be; they are simple to follow. Having good eyesight – or good glasses – and good lighting will make counting easier.

Each square on the chart represents one stitch. However, you will be stitching across the threads of the canvas, so it is the threads that you will count. Each new colour is represented by a number and a key is provided to assist you.

It is best to start stitching in the centre and work outwards.

MAKING YOUR OWN CHARTS

While there are a number of projects here for you to enjoy, it is good to remember that you can convert almost any patchwork design into your own embroidery chart.

Decide how large you want your finished piece to be. This is done by drawing your design onto graph paper, using straight ruled lines (Fig. 2). If you are using 25-count Congress cloth, you will count the number of squares of the graph you have covered with your design, then divide by ten and that will give you the size of your work in centimetres. Dividing by twenty-five will give the size in inches.

Some adjustments may be needed. I have not used as many blocks in the canvas-work pieces as I have in the patchwork, because the work can become unnecessarily complex. These needlepoint pictures are about having fun, so I kept them small.

When you are satisfied with the design, work across the graph paper changing your straight lines into a chart that is readable for embroidery (Fig. 3). For a more detailed explanation, see page 42.

One thing to keep in mind is that, if you are using a design with triangles, it is best to work with an odd number of squares in your basic block, as this will give you a nice point for your triangle.

BLOCKING THE CANVAS

As all the stitches fall in the same direction, a small amount of distortion of the finished embroidery is inevitable. This can be corrected by blocking.

Attach a cloth onto a rigid board. Re-move the embroidery from the frame and place it face down on the cloth. Begin nailing or stapling the embroidery to the board. Wet the embroidery and ensure that as you attach it to the board, you are making perfect 90-degree corners. Leave the embroidery on the board for a day or so until it is dry; it is then ready to be framed.

Another way to block an embroidery which I have recently discovered, is to use a special tape which is available at picture framers. This tape is laid out on foam-core board and the embroidery is pressed into the tape, right side up. Because it is so strong, you will be able to correct the distortion as you go. At the same time, your work is immediately ready for framing.

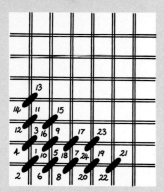

Fig. 1

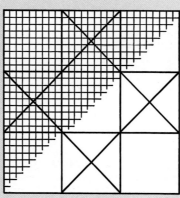

Fig. 2

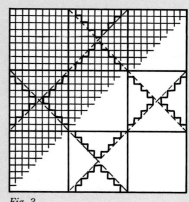

Fig. 3

A Blaze of Stars

I fell in love with this collection of fabrics when they came on the market some years ago. I bought a charm pack, along with some larger pieces for the borders and lattices. Although the exact fabrics may not be on sale in your local patchwork shop, with the fantastic variety of fabrics now available, you should have fun selecting your own!

The quilt itself was a simple design, so this was a good place to try converting a quilt design to embroidery. The fabric colours were my guide for the embroidery, so colour selection was quite easy.

Machine-pieced, hand-quilted
Finished size of quilt: 146 cm × 180 cm (57 in × 71 in)
Finished size of block: 27 cm (10.5 in)
Finished size of embroidery (before framing): 12 cm (5 in) square

'A Blaze of Stars', machine-pieced, hand-quilted by CS, 1991

CONSTRUCTING THE QUILT
Note: You will need to make twenty blocks.

Cutting the blocks
For each block, you will need:
- 4 black squares. Cut a strip across the black fabric 10.5 cm (4 in) wide. Without disturbing the layers of fabric, cut the strips into 10.5 cm (4 in) squares.
- 8 black quarter-square triangles. Cut 12.5 cm (4¾ in) wide strips across the width of the fabric. Without disturbing the layers of fabric, cut the strips into 12.5 cm (4¾ in) squares, then cut across both diagonals.
- 8 coloured quarter-square triangles. Cut at least eight triangles of the same colour for each block. With the fabric doubled, cut a 12.5 cm (4¾ in) square, then cut it across both diagonals.
- 1 coloured square. Cut a 10.5 cm (4 in) square from a variety of fabrics.

Assembling the block
1 Lay out each block as you go (Fig. 1).
2 Chain-piece the coloured quarter-square triangles to the black quarter-square triangles, using a 7.5 mm (¼ in) seam allowance (Fig. 2). Press the seam towards the black triangles.
3 Join these pieces together into squares (Fig. 3). Make sure you butt the seams to get perfect joins at the centre of the square. Press.
4 Lay out the three rows for each block and join the squares into strips (Fig. 4).

YOU WILL NEED
For the quilt
- variety of fabrics for the stars
- 2 m (2¼ yd) of black fabric
- 1.2 m (1⅓ yd) of fabric for the lattice
- 1 m (1⅛ yd) of fabric for the border
- 4 m (4⅓ yd) of fabric for the backing
- 155 cm × 190 cm (61 in × 75 in) of wadding
- 50 cm (20 in) of fabric for the bindings
- black thread
- rotary cutter and mat
- quilter's ruler

For the embroidery
- DMC Stranded Cotton, 2 skeins each: 310, 798
- DMC Stranded Cotton, 1 skein each: 208, 321, 335, 517, 552, 676, 722, 782, 783, 791, 820, 992, 996, 3328
- 20 cm (8 in) square of Congress cloth
- tapestry needle, no. 26
- tapestry frame

5 Press the seams of rows 1 and 3 in the same direction and of row 2 in the opposite direction.
6 Join rows 1 and 2, butting the seams. Add row 3. Press the block.
7 Make up all the blocks in this way.

Assembling the quilt
1 Cut lattice pieces 6.5 cm (2½ in) wide and the length of each block. You will need forty-nine. The lattice pieces surround the blocks, forming the first border.
2 Cut joining 6.5 cm (2½ in) black squares. You will need thirty.
3 Assemble the quilt, following the diagram below.

For the borders
Note: You might like to have the corner square in a different fabric as I have or just take the borders right to the edge.
1 Cut four black 12 cm (4½ in) squares. Cut the borders 12 cm (4½ in) wide and the required length.
2 Add the top and bottom borders first. Press the seams towards the borders.
3 Measure the required length for the side borders, taking into acount the corner squares. Join the four corner squares to the side borders (Fig. 6).
4 Sew the side borders to the quilt top. Press the seams towards the borders.

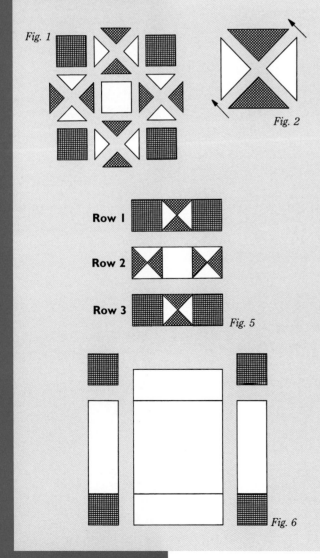

Fig. 1

Fig. 2

Fig. 3

Fig. 4

Row 1

Row 2

Row 3

Fig. 5

Fig. 6

Quilt diagram

'A Blaze of Stars', stitched by CS, 1993

TO FINISH

1 Lay out the backing fabric (face down), the wadding and the quilt top (face up). Pin or tack all the layers in place.

2 I quilted a cross in each square with a 'rope' pattern in the borders.

3 Add bindings, following the instructions on page 9.

4 Attach a label.

STITCHING THE EMBROIDERY

Using three strands of DMC Stranded Cotton, complete the embroidery, following the chart. See page 11 for stitching instructions.

119 x 119 stitches

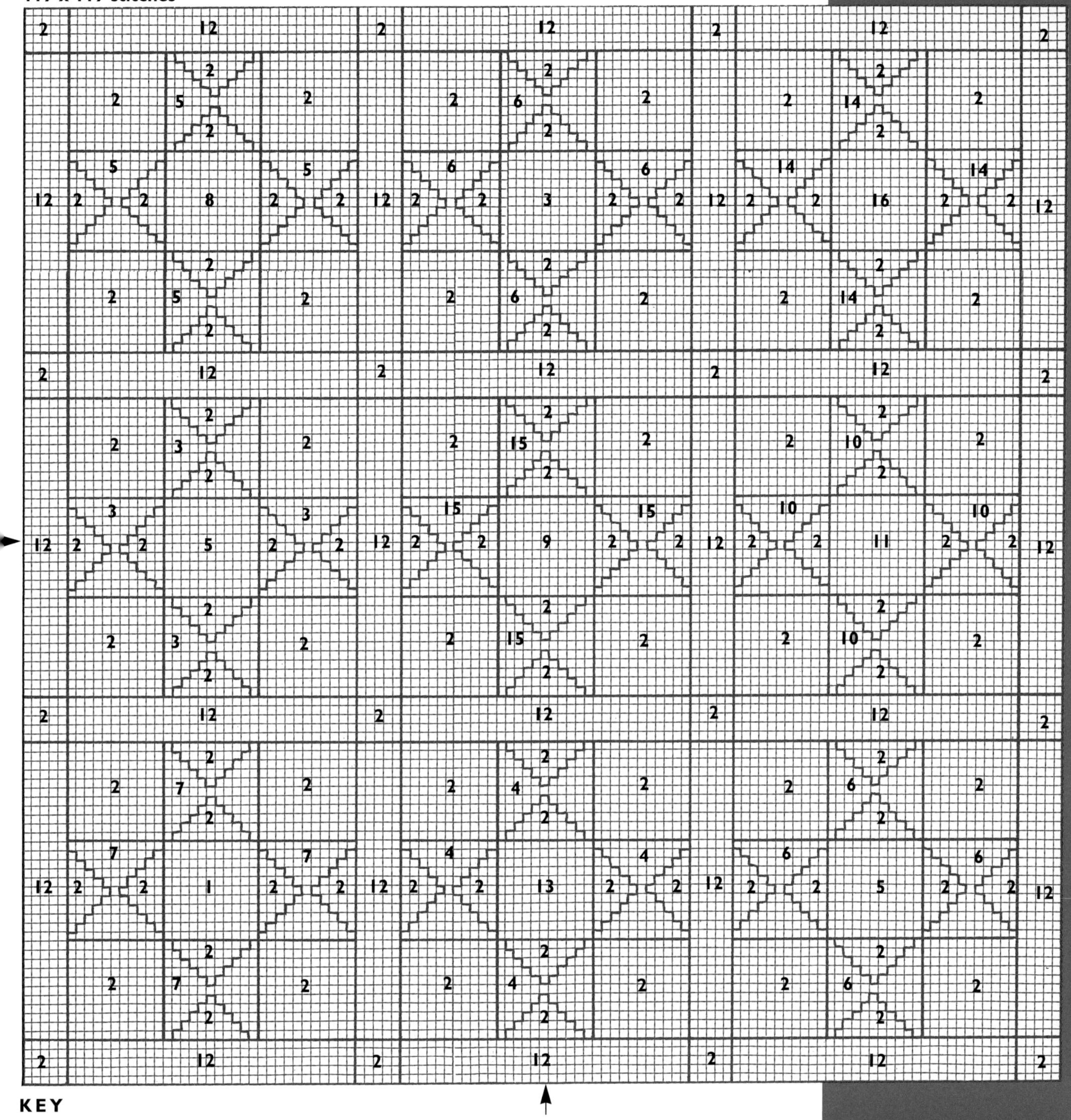

KEY

DMC Stranded Cotton

1 – 208	9 – 782
2 – 310	10 – 783
3 – 321	11 – 791
4 – 335	12 – 798
5 – 517	13 – 820
6 – 552	14 – 992
7 – 676	15 – 996
8 – 722	16 – 3328

Lovable Linda

For the quilt
- 2 m (2¼ yd) of a dark neutral print fabric
- variety of dark and light tone-on-tone pairs of print fabrics
- 70 cm (27 in) of fabric for the lattice
- 50 cm (20 in) of dark pink fabric for the first border and the small lattice joiners
- 20–50 cm (8–20 in) of at least four fabrics for the last border
- thread to match
- rotary cutter and mat
- quilter's ruler
- 5 m (5½ yd) of fabric for the backing
- 60 cm (24 in) of fabric for the bindings
- 175 cm x 215 cm (69 in x 85 in) of wadding

For the embroidery
- 25 cm (10 in) square of Congress cloth
- DMC Stranded Cotton, 4 skeins, 3799
- DMC Stranded Cotton, 1 skein of each: 210, 333, 351, 601, 718, 731, 742, 798, 800, 3341, 3608, 3811, 3812, 3819
- tapestry needle, no. 26
- tapestry frame

The block I used for this quilt was one that I was not acquainted with until I found it in an old book that my husband bought in a secondhand bookshop in the United States.

The book was printed in the early seventies and seems quite old-fashioned compared to today's wonderful array of books. It has a hand-written inscription in the front 'To Our Lovable Linda, New York City, Christmas 1976', and is now a treasured volume in my library. Maybe, my daughter, Linda, will enjoy it one day!

Machine-pieced, hand-quilted
Finished size of quilt: 167 cm x 202 cm (66 in x 80 in)
Finished size of block: 31 cm (13 in)
Finished size of embroidery: 15 cm (6 in) square

CONSTRUCTING THE QUILT
Cutting the blocks
Note: There are twenty blocks. For each block, you will need to select pairs of light and dark tone-on-tone fabrics and cut:
- one 13.5 cm (5½ in) square of the light print fabric for the centre
- four 7.5 cm (3 in) squares of the dark print fabric for connector squares
- 4 half-square triangles of the dark neutral print fabric. Cut 8.5 cm (3⅜ in) strips from selvage to selvage of the dark neutral print fabric. Cut the strip into 8.5 cm (3⅜ in) squares. Cut across one diagonal.
- 4 half-square triangles of the light print fabric. Cut 8.5 cm (3⅜ in) squares, then cut them across one diagonal.
- 16 quarter-square triangles of the light print fabric. Cut four 9.5 cm (3¾ in) squares, layer them, then cut across both diagonals.
- 16 quarter-square triangles of the dark print fabric. Cut four 9.5 cm (3¾ in) squares, layer them, then cut across both

diagonals to yield sixteen triangles.
- 4 border strips of the dark neutral print fabric – 2 pieces 5 cm x 25.5 cm (2 in x 10½ in) and 2 pieces 5 cm x 32.5 cm (2 in x 13½ in).

Assembling the block
1 Chain-piece the quarter-square triangles (Fig. 1). Press the seams towards the dark fabric.
2 Join these pieces together to form squares (Fig. 2). Butt the seams for perfect joins at the centre. Press.
3 Join these squares together to form the units at the side of the block (Fig. 3).
4 Join the corner half-square triangles (Fig. 4). Press the seams towards the dark fabric.
5 Lay the first connector square on a corner of the centre square, right sides together. Stitch across the diagonal. Trim the excess fabric from the connector square only (Fig. 5). Do not cut away the centre square as this maintains the base square. You will be left with two thicknesses of fabric. Save these scraps for your next miniature quilt. Press the connector square back over the seam. Complete the other three corners in the same way.

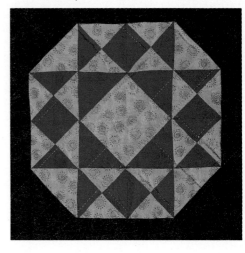

**Above: 'Lovable Linda', machine-pieced,
hand-quilted by CS, 1997
Left: Detail of a block**

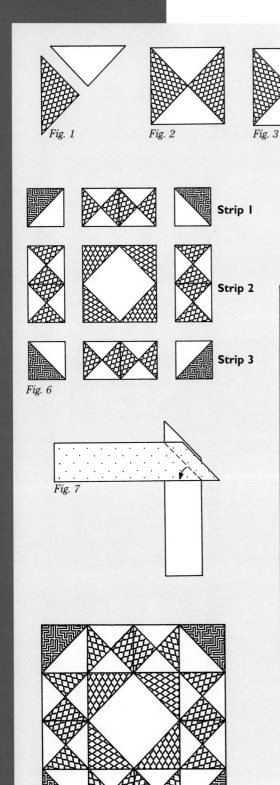

Fig. 1

Fig. 2

Fig. 3

Fig. 4

Fig. 5

Strip 1

Strip 2

Strip 3

Fig. 6

Fig. 7

Block Diagram

Quilt Diagram

6 Lay out the pieces for each block (Fig. 6).

7 Join the pieces into strips. Press the seams of Strips 1 and 3 in the same direction and the seams of Strip 2 in the opposite direction. Join the strips, butting the seams and making sure all the points are accurate.

8 Make up all the blocks in the same way.

9 Attach the short borders to the sides of the block. Press the seams towards the borders. Attach the longer pieces to the top and bottom of the block. Press the seams towards the borders.

Assembling the blocks

1 Cut lattice pieces 5 cm × 32.5 cm (2 in × 13½ in). You will need thirty-one.

2 Cut 5 cm (2 in) joining squares.

3 Lay out the whole quilt, following the quilt diagram. Assemble the blocks into rows, then join the rows.

For the borders

1 Cut the first dark pink border 5 cm (2 in) wide. Sew the borders to the sides first, then to the top and bottom.

2 Cut the 5 cm (2 in) wide second borders from the dark neutral print. Add them to the quilt, as for the first borders.

3 Cut the 10 cm (4 in) wide third border from four different fabrics. To make the diagonal joins, cut the ends of two adjoining strips at an angle of 45 degrees, using the 45 degree marking on your ruler. Make sure the cuts point in the right direction. Lay the fabrics with the right sides facing and with the 7.5 mm (¼ in) seam allowance protruding at each end (Fig. 7). Stitch, then press the seams open.

TO FINISH

1 Lay out the backing fabric (face down), the wadding and the quilt top (face up). Pin or tack all the layers together.

2 This quilt was hand-quilted with evenly spaced lines that come to a point. There is really no pattern; just start marking lines and off you go.

3 Add bindings, following the general instructions for binding on page 9.

4 Attach a label.

STITCHING THE EMBROIDERY

See the embroidery chart on page 22. Using three strands of DMC Stranded Cotton, complete the embroidery as charted. See page 11 for stitching instructions.

'Lovable Linda', stitched by CS, 1997

135 x 135 stitches

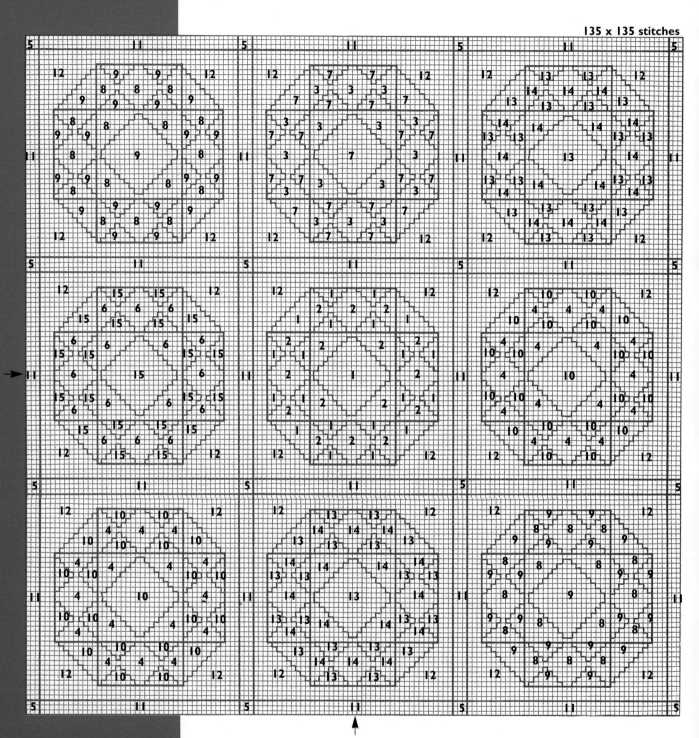

KEY
DMC Stranded Cotton

1 – 210	9 – 800
2 – 333	10 – 3341
3 – 351	11 – 3608
4 – 601	12 – 3799
5 – 718	13 – 3811
6 – 731	14 – 3812
7 – 742	15 – 3819
8 – 798	

Blue Medallion

I particularly like medallion quilts because of their distinct focus. In this quilt the arrangement of the Ohio Star blocks is the focus. The challenge of medallion quilts is also fun, because the measurements have to be so exact to make each successive round fit. The interesting fabrics are part of the joy of this quilt for me. When I bought the yellow and blue checked fabric, my non-quilting friend was aghast, thinking no-one could do anything with it, but I really think it works well here!

Machine-pieced, hand-quilted
Finished size of quilt: 182 cm (72 in) square
Finished size of block: 24 cm (9 in)
Finished size of embroidery: 11.5 cm (4½ in) square

'Blue Medallion', machine-pieced, hand-quilted by CS, 1995

CONSTRUCTING THE QUILT
Cutting the Ohio Star blocks

1 You will need five Ohio Star blocks, using two different fabrics for each block. For each block, you will need:
- one 9.5 cm (3½ in) centre square from the star fabric
- four 9.5 cm (3½ in) corner squares from the background fabric
- two 11.5 cm (4¼ in) squares (cut with the fabric doubled) from the star and the background fabric. Without disturbing the layers, cut the squares across both diagonals to yield 8 triangles from each fabric.
2 Lay out each block as you go (Fig. 1).
3 Chain-piece the quarter-square triangles into pairs, using a 7.5 mm (¼ in) seam allowance. Press the seams towards the background fabric.
4 Join these pieces together to make squares. Butt the seams to get perfect joins at the centre. Press well.
5 Lay out the three rows for each block (Fig. 2), then join the squares into strips (Fig. 3).
6 Press the seams of strips 1 and 3 in the same direction and of strip 2, the opposite way.
7 Join strips 1 and 2, butting the seams. Add strip 3. Press the block well.

Making up the centre

1 For the four dark triangles around the Ohio Stars, cut two 26.5 cm (9⅞ in) squares. Cut each across one diagonal to yield four triangles.

YOU WILL NEED
For the quilt
- rotary cutter and mat
- quilter's ruler
- fabrics for the five Ohio Star blocks in the centre
- light and dark filler fabric that surrounds the Ohio Star blocks
- fabric for the Nine-patch blocks
- fabric for the half-square triangles
- fabric for the pinwheels
- 50 cm (20 in) of fabric for the first non-pieced border
- 50 cm (20 in) of fabric for the second non-pieced border
- 1 m (1¼ yd) of fabric for the third non-pieced border
- 4 m (4⅓ yd) of fabric for the backing
- matching sewing thread
- 190 cm (75 in) square of wadding
- 60 cm (24 in) of fabric for the bindings

For the embroidery
- DMC Stranded Cotton, 2 skeins each: 796, 798
- DMC Stranded Cotton, 1 skein each: 341, 402, 783, 800, 809, 977, 3753, 3778, 3821
- 20 cm (8 in) square of Congress cloth
- tapestry needle, no. 26
- tapestry frame

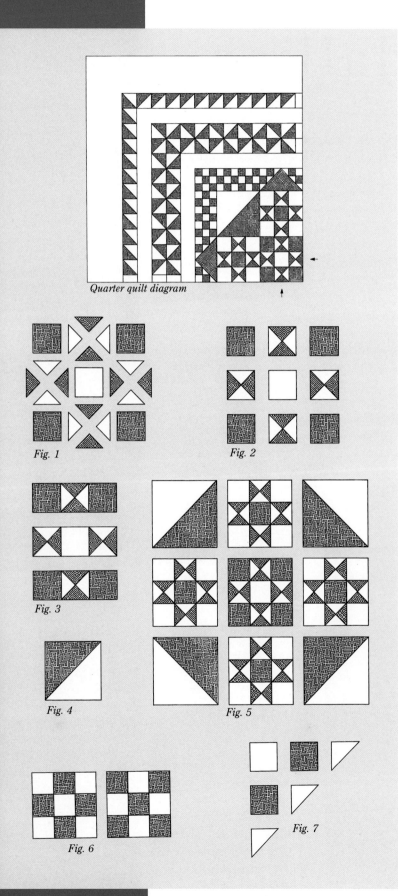

Quarter quilt diagram

Fig. 1

Fig. 2

Fig. 3

Fig. 4

Fig. 5

Fig. 6

Fig. 7

2 For the four light triangles that surround the Ohio Stars, cut two 26.5 cm (9⅞ in) squares). Cut each square across one diagonal to yield four triangles.

3 Join the light and dark triangles into four squares, light on one side, dark on the other (Fig. 4). Press the seams towards the dark fabric.

4 Assemble the centre medallion in the same way as for the Ohio Star blocks, except on a larger scale (Fig. 5).

Making the Nine-patch round

1 Before starting the nine patches, you will need to cut the points of the centre medallion as these are incorporated into this round. Using the same dark fabric that surrounds your Ohio Star blocks, cut a 27.5 cm (10¼ in) square. Cut across both diagonals to yield four triangles. Set them aside.

2 Cut a variety of light and dark 5.5 cm (2 in) squares – 96 light and 108 dark.

3 Join the squares into Nine-patch blocks. You will need twelve with dark corners and eight with light corners (Fig. 6).

4 Make eight half Nine-patch blocks with light corners to go on either side of the dark points of the centre medallion. Cut six 6.5 cm (2⅜ in) squares of light fabric and cut them across one diagonal to yield twelve triangles. Assemble these half blocks using the diagram (Fig. 7).

5 To make up the full round of Nine-patch blocks, assemble them as shown in the diagram. Make two of figure 8 and two of figure 9.

6 Attach these strips to the centre square, by joining the shorter ones to opposite sides of the centre square. Press, then join the two longer ones to the other two sides. Press.

First unpieced border

Cut two strips 9.5 cm x 97.5 cm (3½ in x 36½ in). Attach them to opposite sides. Make sure these measurements are correct by measuring each side of the quilt. There may be some discrepancy. Cut two strips 9.5 cm x 113.5 cm (3½ in x 42½ in) and

attach them to the other two sides. Make sure these measurements are correct by measuring each side of the quilt. There may be some discrepancy.

Pinwheel border

Note: You will need to make thirty-two pinwheel blocks, each one made up of four light and four dark half-square triangles.

1 From both the light and dark fabrics, cut sixty-four 10.5 cm (3⅞ in) squares (fabric doubled). Cut across one diagonal. You will need 128 dark and 128 light half-square triangles.
2 Chain-piece the light and dark half-square triangles into squares. Press the seams towards the dark fabrics (Fig. 10).
3 Join four squares into Pinwheel blocks (Fig. 11). Your accuracy will be improved, if you use the three-pin method at the centre (see page 7).
4 Join seven Pinwheel blocks in a row, twice (Fig. 12). Add them to the top and bottom of the quilt. Press.
5 Join nine Pinwheel blocks in a row (twice). Add them to the quilt sides.

Second unpieced border

1 Cut two strips 9.5 cm x 145.5 cm (3½ in x 54½ in) and join them to the top and bottom. Press. Make sure these measurements are correct by measuring

each side of the quilt. There may be some discrepancy.

2 Cut two strips 9.5 cm x 161.5 cm (3½ in x 60½ in) and join them to the sides of the quilt. Press. Make sure these measurements are correct by measuring each side of the quilt. There may be some discrepancy.

Half-square triangle border

1 Cut a variety of fabrics into a total of eighty 10.5 cm (3⅞ in) squares. Cut them across one diagonal to yield 160 half-square triangles.
2 Chain-piece the triangles into squares (Fig. 13). Press.
3 Join nineteen squares into a strip. Add it to the top. Repeat for the bottom. Press.
4 Join twenty-one squares into a strip. Add it to one side. Press. Repeat for the other side.

Third unpieced border

1 Measure the width of the quilt and cut two 12 cm (5 in) wide borders to this length. Join them to the top and bottom of the quilt.
2 Measure the length of the quilt, including the top and bottom borders. Cut two 12 cm (5 in) wide borders to this length and add them to the sides. Press.

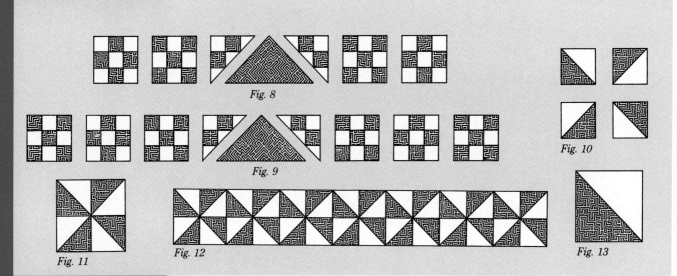

Fig. 8

Fig. 9

Fig. 10

Fig. 11

Fig. 12

Fig. 13

TO FINISH

1 Lay out the backing fabric (face down), the wadding, then the quilt top (face upwards). Pin or baste all the layers in place.
2 This quilt was quilted with a variety of patterns: circles, a square grid in the centre and a diagonal grid in the outer borders.
3 Add the bindings, following the general instructions on page 9.
4 Attach a label.

'Blue Medallion', stitched by CS, 1997

Left: Detail of the quilt

113 x 113 stitches

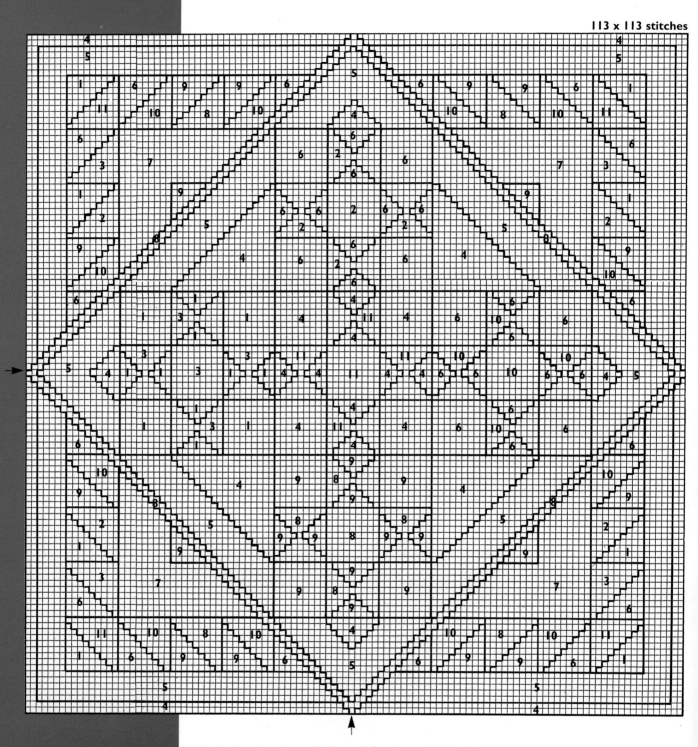

STITCHING THE EMBROIDERY

Using three strands of DMC Stranded Cotton, complete the embroidery following the chart. See page 11 for stitching instructions.

KEY

DMC Stranded Cotton

1 – 341	7 – 809
2 – 402	8 – 977
3 – 783	9 – 3753
4 – 796	10 – 3778
5 – 798	11 – 3821
6 – 800	

Watercolour

My first quiltmaking experience was at the New South Wales Embroiderers' Guild when I wanted to make a cot cover for a friend's new baby. There, I was taught the English-piecing method, a very good beginning for someone who enjoys hand-sewing. I love the accuracy of English-piecing.

Traditional English patchwork relies on the use of a metal template which is used to cut cards onto which the fabrics are stitched. These templates are not always easy to find, so I use the rotary cutter to cut the cards that are needed. This method works well for the simple square and half-square triangle required for this project. For a more complex project that uses hexagons, you really do need to find those metal templates.

Hand-pieced and hand-quilted
Finished size of quilt: 49 cm (19½ in) square
Finished size of embroidery: 11.5 cm (4½ in) square

CONSTRUCTING THE QUILT

Preparing the cards
1　Cut the cardboard into 2.5 cm (1 in) squares, using the rotary cutter. Accuracy is essential. You will need 168 squares.
2　Cut more 2.5 cm (1 in) squares across one diagonal to make half-square triangles. You will need 128.

Cutting the fabric
Note: The cards are all the finished size. Seam allowances must be added to the fabric, as you cut it out.
1　From the light fabrics, cut eighty-four 4 cm (1½ in) squares.
2　From the dark fabrics, cut eighty-four 4 cm (1½ in) squares.

3　Cut 64 light and 64 dark triangles that are 7.5 mm (¼ in) larger than the cardboard pieces. The best way to do this is to cut a master template. Trace one of the triangle cardboard pieces onto heavier card and add a 7.5 mm (¼ in) all around. Cut it out for a master template for cutting the fabric triangles (Fig. 1).

Assembling the blocks
1　Hold the template to the wrong side of the fabric with the 7.5 mm (¼ in) seam allowances showing all around. Using the medium, sharp needle and basting thread, begin with a good starting knot and baste the fabric to the template, turning the seam allowances over the edge (Fig. 2). Stitch only the seam allowances. Ensure you have nice tight points at the corners, although the seam allowances will protrude beyond the template. Do not worry as they will not show, when you stitch the pieces

'Watercolour', hand-pieced, hand-quilted by CS, 1996

YOU WILL NEED
For the quilt
- variety of dark and light floral fabrics
- lightweight cardboard (used greeting cards work well)
- 20 cm (8 in) of very dark fabric for the inner border
- 20 cm (8 in) of floral fabric for the outer border
- rotary cutter and mat
- quilter's ruler
- thread to match
- basting thread
- 60 cm (24 in) square of fabric for the backing
- 60 cm (24 in) square of wadding
- 20 cm (8 in) of fabric for the bindings
- good quality medium and fine, sharp needles

For the embroidery
- 20 cm (8 in) square of Congress cloth
- DMC Stranded Cotton, 1 skein each of a range of light colours: 211, 353, 504, 745, 928, 948, 955, 963, 964, 3609, 3689, 3743, 3747
- DMC Stranded Cotton, 1 skein each of a range of dark colours: 208, 352, 502, 518, 552, 743, 809, 899, 912, 952, 3607, 3778, 3806
- tapestry needle, no. 26
- tapestry frame

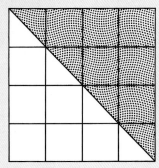

Block diagram

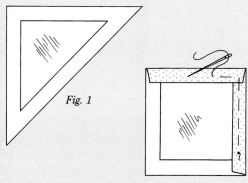

Fig. 1

Fig. 2

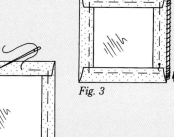

Fig. 3

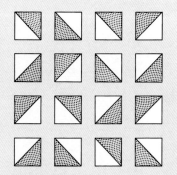

Quilt diagram

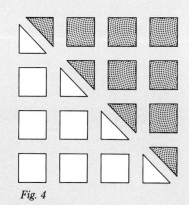

Fig. 4

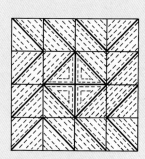

Quilting diagram

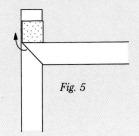

Fig. 5

together. Maintain the proper tension. Too loose and your work will be floppy and inaccurate. Too tight and the template will bend out of shape. Baste all the squares and triangles over the cards.

2 Take two fabric-covered templates and hold them, right sides together, with the corners matching. Using the fine sharp needle and a thread that matches the fabrics, start topstitching 7.5 mm (¼ in) from the corner and stitch towards the nearest corner. Take a stitch that connects the points, then work back across the whole side. Stitch carefully into the corner, then stitch back over your sewing for another 7.5 mm (¼ in) (Fig. 3). You have now stitched twice near the corners and this means there is no need for knots, which add unnecessary bulk. When topstitching,

only pick up the fabric, do not sew into the card.

3   You will need sixteen blocks, each of which has twelve light squares, twelve dark squares, four light triangles and four dark triangles (Fig. 4).

4   Topstitch the light triangles to the dark triangles making four squares.

5   Topstitch the squares into strips, then topstitch four strips together, making sure all the points match (Fig. 5). This is best done starting and ending at each corner, rather than working across the row without breaks.

6   Stitch the blocks together, following the quilt diagram.

7   With the cards still in place, press the quilt lightly on both sides. Remove the cards from the centre, leaving them in place around the outside edge. The templates can be used in your next quilt.

For the borders

1   For the narrow border, cut four pieces 2 cm x 43 cm (¾ in x 17 in).

2   For the wider border, cut four pieces 4 cm x 55 cm (1½ in x 20 in).

3   Pin a narrow border to a wide border, matching centres. Stitch. Complete for all four borders. I used the machine here, but continue to hand-stitch if you wish.

4   Press under a 7.5 mm (¼ in) seam allowance on each of the narrow border pieces and topstitch this to the quilt, matching the centre of the border with the centre of the quilt edge. The cards in the outer edge of the quilt will make the stitching easier. Complete for all four borders, leaving openings at the corners, then remove the last of the cards.

5   At each corner, lay one of the corner extensions flat. Lay the other corner across it, folded back at an angle of 45 degrees. From the front of the quilt, match all the seams and pin, making sure you have a perfect point at the corner (Fig. 5). From the back, trim the excess fabric. Baste, then hem the corner accurately from the front.

TO FINISH

1   Lay out the backing fabric (face down), the wadding and the quilt top (face up). Pin or baste all the layers together.

2   This quilt was hand-quilted in a series of lines, working from corner to corner of all the small squares in the blocks.

3   Add the bindings, following the general instructions on page 9.

4   Attach a label.

'Lollipop', stitched by CS, 1997

112 x 112 stitches

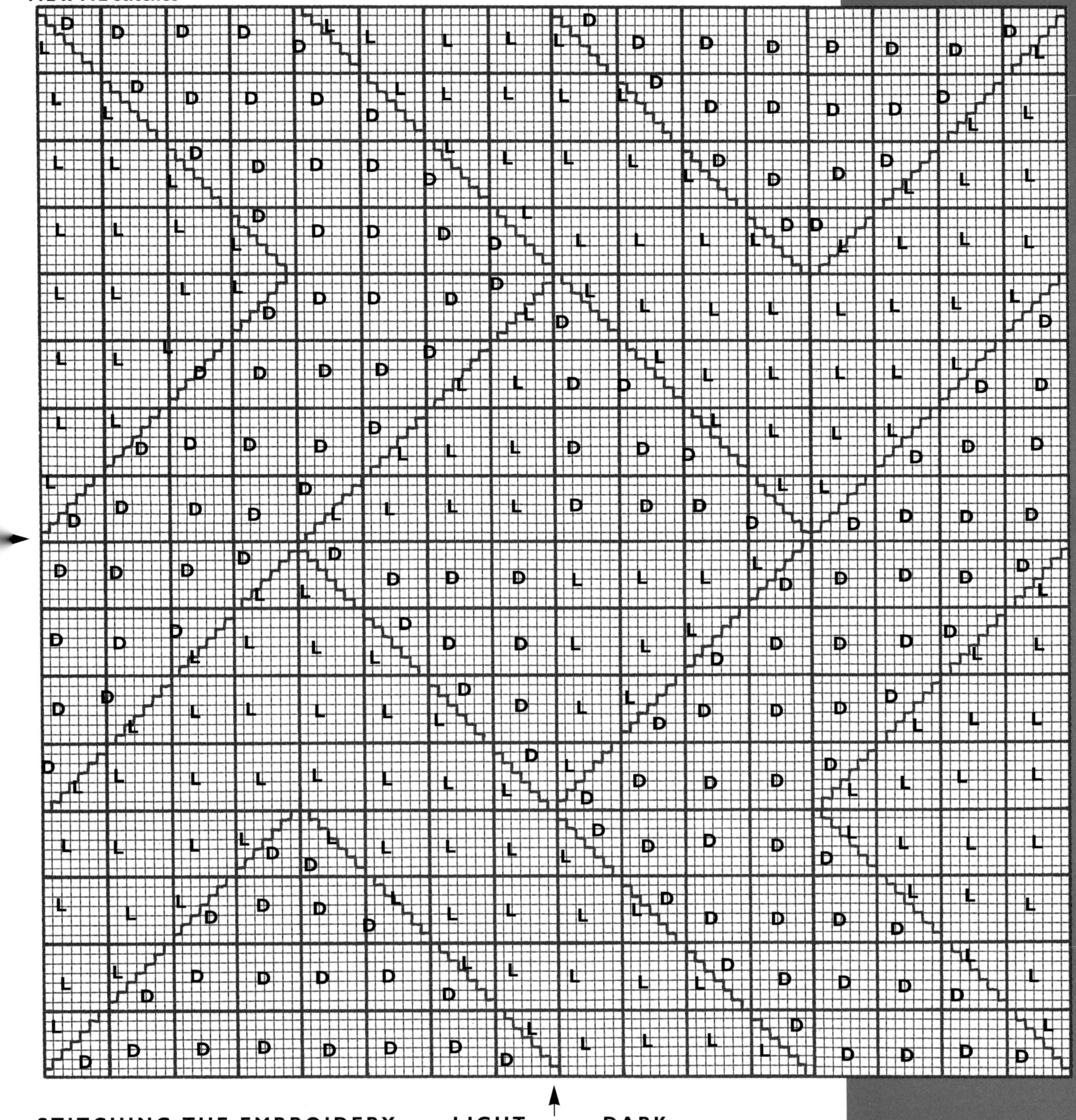

STITCHING THE EMBROIDERY

Using three strands of DMC Stranded Cotton, complete the embroidery as charted. Individual colours are not specified in this chart, rather areas are shown where you should use the light (L) or dark (D) ranges of threads. Have fun putting them anywhere you like!

LIGHT		DARK	
211	963	208	899
353	964	352	912
504	3609	502	952
745	3689	518	3607
928	3743	552	3778
948	3747	743	3806
955		809	

Central Space

YOU WILL NEED

For the quilt

- 1.8 m (2 yd) of deep navy or black fabric for the background
- 25 cm (10 in) of plain coloured fabric in each of light, medium and dark shades of each colour
- dark thread to match
- rotary cutter and mat
- quilter's ruler
- 3 m (3⅓ yd) of fabric for the backing
- 145 cm x 170 cm (57 in x 67 in) of wadding
- 50 cm (20 in) of fabric for the bindings

For the embroidery

- 20 cm (8 in) square of Congress cloth
- DMC Stranded Cotton, 2 skeins, 823
- DMC Stranded Cotton, 1 skein each: 333, 340, 341, 500, 550, 552, 554, 747, 909, 912, 915, 943, 955, 959, 995, 996, 3607, 3609, 3685, 3687, 3688, 3808, 3810, 3811
- tapestry needle, size 26
- tapestry frame

Colour is the first thing you notice about 'Central Space'. I spent a good part of 1997 hand-dyeing my own fabrics to create a range of values for each colour. This quilt requires three shades of as many colours as you can find. I used nine different colours, then spent time balancing those colours across the quilt to give an Amish feel to the finished work.

An Ohio Star is the basic block, but the central filler between each block makes for a more complex design.

Machine-pieced, hand-quilted
Finished size of quilt: 132 cm x 158 cm (52 in x 62 in)
Finished size of block: 25.5 cm (10½ in)
Finished size of embroidery: 11.5 cm (4½ in) square

CONSTRUCTING THE QUILT

Note: You will need to make twenty Ohio Star blocks and twelve joining blocks.

Cutting the Ohio Star blocks

Note: For each Ohio Star block, you will need to cut light, medium and dark values of each colour as well as the background colour. For most of my blocks, I cut dark centres, surrounded by medium and ending with light points. Notice that I reversed the light and dark on three of the blocks. For each block, cut:

- one 10 cm (4 in) centre square in a dark shade.
- 4 background quarter-square triangles. It is best to cut these for the whole quilt in one go. Cut 12 cm (4¾ in) wide strips from selvage to selvage, then

cut the strips into squares. Without moving the layers of fabric, cut across both diagonals. You will need 80 of the quarter-square triangles for the whole quilt.

- 8 light-coloured quarter-square triangles. Cut two 12 cm (4¾ in) squares, then cut them across both diagonals.
- 4 medium-coloured quarter-square triangles. Cut one 12 cm (4¾ in) square, then cut it across both diagonals.

Assembling the Ohio Star block

1 Lay out each block as you go (Fig. 1).
2 Chain-piece the quarter-square triangles, press the seam towards the background fabric (Fig. 2).
3 Join these triangles together to make squares. Butt the seams to get perfect joins at the centre of your square. Press, then lay out the block again to

'Central Space', machine-pieced, hand-quilted by CS, 1997

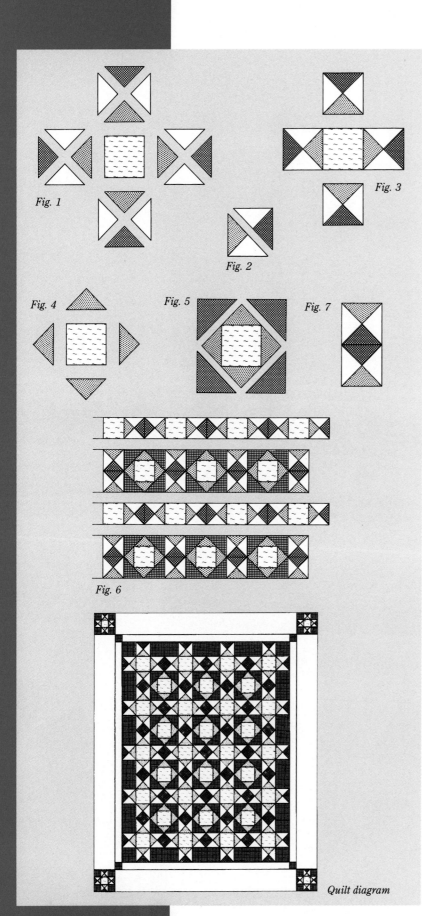

Fig. 1

Fig. 2

Fig. 3

Fig. 4

Fig. 5

Fig. 7

Fig. 6

Quilt diagram

check that you have pieced it accurately.

4 Join the three squares across the middle (Fig. 3). Press.

5 Pin the three pieces and set them aside. Repeat these steps for the other nineteen blocks, trying to get an even balance of colours.

Cutting the joining blocks

Note: For each of the twelve joining blocks, you must still consider colour balance. You will need the background colour and the dark and medium value of your selected colours.

For each of the blocks, cut:

• one 10 cm (4 in) square from the dark value fabric.

• 4 quarter-square triangles from the medium value fabric. Cut two 12 cm (4¾ in) squares, then cut them across both diagonals.

• 4 half-square triangles from the background fabric. Cut two 11 cm (4⅜ in) squares, then cut them across one diagonal.

Assembling the joining blocks

1 Stitch the medium-value triangles to the dark centre square (Fig. 4). Press the seams towards the square.

2 Add the four background triangles (Fig. 5). Press the seams towards the background fabric.

Assembling the quilt

1 Lay out all the pieces on the floor or a design wall to get a good balance of colour. They can be pinned to a white sheet, then pinned or taped to the wall.

2 When you have laid out all the blocks, you will have pieces missing along the edges and corners (Fig. 6). These are completed in background colour. For the corners, cut four 10 cm (4 in) squares and put them in place.

3 For the side pieces, cut three 10 cm (4 in) wide strips of background colour from selvage to selvage. Open out the strips and cut fourteen 18.5 cm (7½ in)

lengths. Put them in place to complete your layout.

4   Join all the pieces for each Strip 1, keeping all the colours in their correct position. Press all the seams in the same direction. Work slowly putting each piece back in its rightful place before you pick up the next one.

5   For each Strip 2, join together the vertical star point pieces (Fig. 7). Press.

6   Join all the pieces across each Strip 2, keeping all the colours in their rightful place. Press all the seams for the Strip 2 in the opposite direction to Strip 1.

7   Join all the strips together making sure that points match. Use the three-pin method explained on page 7. If you have pressed the strips correctly, your seams will be going in opposite directions; this will assist your accuracy.

For the borders

1   Make four different-coloured Ohio Star blocks for the corners, as before. For each of these, you will need to cut:
- four 5.5 cm (2 in) squares of background colour.
- one 5.5 m (2 in) squares of the dark value fabric.
- 4 quarter-square triangles of the medium value fabric. Cut a 7.5 cm (2¾ in) square across both diagonals.
- 4 quarter-square triangles of the background fabric. Cut a 7.5 cm (2¾ in) square across both diagonals.
- 8 quarter-square triangles from the light value fabric. Cut two 7.5 cm (2¾ in) squares across both diagonals.

2   Cut two 5.5 cm (2 in) wide strips from different-coloured medium fabric from selvage to selvage. Cut two 9.5 cm (4 in) wide strips of background fabric. Join the medium strip to the background strip, then join one to the top and bottom of the quilt. Press the seam allowances away from the quilt.

3   Repeat the process for cutting the side borders, using two more medium fabrics. You will need to have joins in these side pieces to make them long enough. Attach an Ohio Star block at each end of these border strips. Take care that the border length measures the same as the quilt side, before you add the Ohio Star blocks. Press. Join the side borders to the quilt top. Press the seams towards the borders.

TO FINISH

1   Lay out the backing fabric (face down), the wadding and the quilt top (face up). Pin or tack all layers in place.

2   This quilt was hand-quilted with a series of evenly spaced interlocking lines that come to a point. There is really no pattern; just start making lines and see how you go.

3   Add bindings, following the general instructions for binding on page 9.

4   Attach a label.

'Central Space' stitched by CS, 1997

99 x 99 stitches

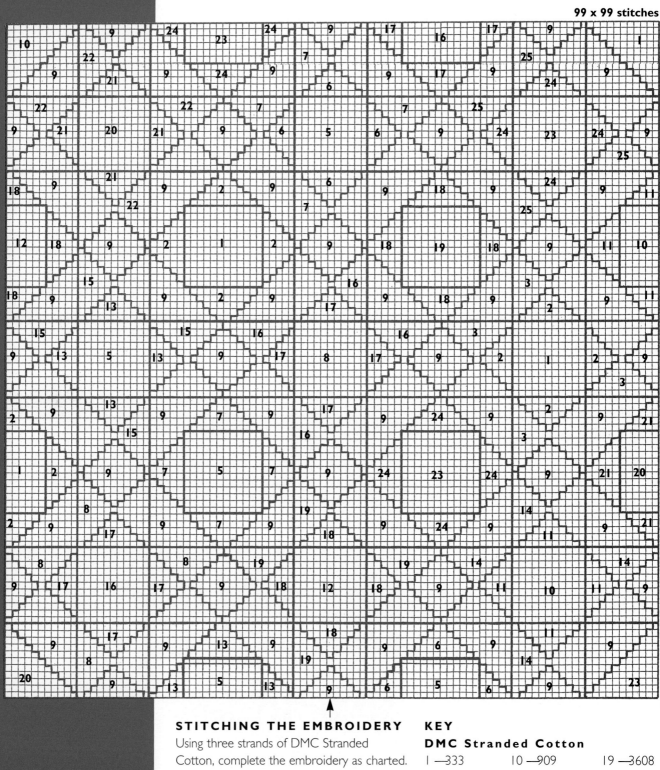

STITCHING THE EMBROIDERY

Using three strands of DMC Stranded
Cotton, complete the embroidery as charted.
See page 11 for stitching instructions.

KEY

DMC Stranded Cotton

1 —333	10 —909	19 —3608
2 —340	11 —912	20 —3685
3 —341	12 —915	21 —3687
4 —500	13 —943	22 —3688
5 —550	14 —955	23 —3808
6 —552	15 —959	24 —3810
7 —554	16 —995	25 —3811
8 —747	17 —996	
9 —823	18 —3607	

Designing Rotated Blocks

Quiltmakers have been designing blocks for many years. It may have been to express something of their daily lives – how many tea cup blocks are there? – or to make a political statement, like Fifty Four Forty or Fight. But design need not stop with these traditional blocks. I have used the traditional block format to create quilts with a contemporary look by drawing simple lines, then rotating them. The result is a new, dynamic design which allows me great opportunities to play with colour.

Drawing your blocks

1   In each of the nine boxes in your enlarged photocopy of figure 1, draw a variety of lines to create interesting shapes. Here are some ideas to get you started:
- Draw some with a diagonal plus any other lines;
- draw some with a number of horizontal lines and one slanted from a corner to a point on an opposite side;
- draw some with verticals;
- draw some with curves and straight lines;
- draw some with parallel lines, horizontal, vertical, diagonal or slanted lines;
- add lines to areas that appear too large;
- draw lines that do not touch the sides at all.
2   Number all of your blocks. Figure 2 shows some of the ideas that I have worked with.
3   When you have filled all the boxes, photocopy the page four times.

Creating whole quilt designs

1   Cut out the four copies of each block separately. Arrange them on a new piece of paper with the first block aligned the way you first drew it. Place another block beside it, but turned through an angle of 90 degrees. Take the third one and place it below the second one, also turned through an angle of 90 degrees. Place the fourth one under the first one, also turned through an angle of 90 degrees. Do this for all nine of your designs (Fig. 3). You will fit a number to a page.

YOU WILL NEED
- an enlarged photocopy of Fig. 1 on page 40
- access to a photocopier (I go to my local library)
- ruler
- pencil
- eraser
- glue stick
- paper scissors
- coloured pencils
- extra A4 sheets of paper

Fig. 1

2 Photocopy these arranged blocks four times each and paste them together. You have already done the rotations, so they will all go together side by side without further rotations.

3 Have a look at your designs. Did they work? If you really think they haven't, then discard them, but do not be too hasty at this stage. Often, something that doesn't work now, may work later. Select one that you really like and make two or three photocopies of it.

4 Colour in the photocopies of your chosen design. There are infinite numbers of ways they can be coloured in. Look for secondary designs which form when the blocks come together. Look at how you can you use these in your quiltmaking. The more colouring in you do, the more inventive your quilts will be.

5 Select some more of your designs, photocopy them and keep colouring! I have included some of my colourings to encourage you.

Note: For the computer literate, the above instructions will be slow. Your computer can do all of this much faster!

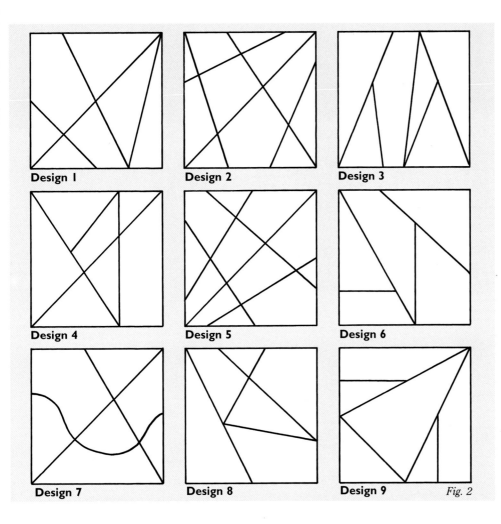

Design 1

Design 2

Design 3

Design 4

Design 5

Design 6

Design 7

Design 8

Design 9

Fig. 2

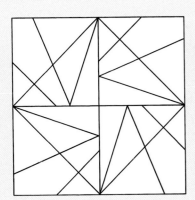

Fig. 3

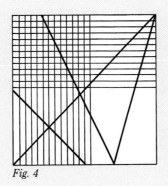
Fig. 4

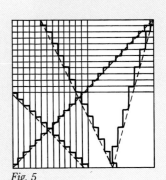
Fig. 5

Translating a Design to Embroidery

YOU WILL NEED

- 2 mm (¹⁄₁₀ in) graph paper
- pencil
- ruler
- eraser
- variety of stranded cottons
- tapestry needle, no. 26
- Congress cloth
- tapestry frame

Experiment with colour until you are satisfied

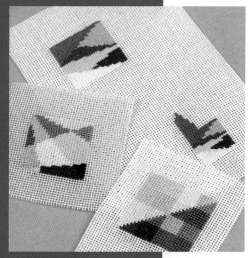

1 In a corner of your sheet of graph paper, draw up your basic block, using straight lines for now. You will need to keep the proportions of your block accurate. I draw the block over twenty-five squares of the graph paper as this seems to work well (Fig. 4, page 41).

2 When you think the proportions look right, trace over the straight lines to show the stitching (Fig. 5, page 41). Where your lines follow a straight line on the graph paper, there is no need to change them. Where your lines cross the lines of the grid, you need to make careful decisions about where to draw each stitch. Each square on your grid represents a stitch. If you are not satisfied with your lines, redraw them until you are.

3 Select a few colours of DMC Stranded Cotton that you are happy to work with and stitch your block on a small piece of canvas. Don't worry about a frame at this stage, you are only stitching a sample to see if it works. If the lines are not straight, amend the chart. It is worth taking this step so that your finished work looks good.

4 When you are satisfied with your block, decide how large you want your embroidery to be. For most of my designs, four repeats of the full rotation were sufficient. This gives one secondary design, as can be seen in 'Floriade Pansies' on page 45. For 'Whirling'' I repeated the block nine times, giving four secondary designs.

5 Stitch the design as you have charted it, in the colours of your choice. Your basic block that you graphed is very useful to refer to when stitching. Pin it to a clear space in the corner of your canvas and turn it each time you start a new square and wish to rotate. This saves working with a large chart. Mark your colour selections on this small graph.

A NOTE ABOUT COLOUR

Colour selection is important and here you have to rely on your own eye. Sometimes I have an idea of what I want, as in 'Floriade Pansies', at other times, I go to my colour reference collection of pictures.

Be prepared to change your mind. Sometimes you can select a colour and it can be quite wrong, when it is placed next to another colour. Combinations can surprise you as to how well they work together. Be prepared to experiment – even if it means working a few practice pieces until you get the colour right. Some examples of my practice pieces are shown on this page.

DMC sells a colour chart of all their stranded cottons which will greatly assist you with colour choices.

Translating a Design to a Quilt

MAKING THE TEMPLATES

You can make your quilt block any size you wish, depending on the desired size of the quilt and how many blocks you want to make. I have chosen 20 cm (8 in) for 'Floriade Pansies' and 'Whirling' because it suited the quilt size I wanted, where 12 cm (5 in) was fine for 'Follow the Shades'.

1 Draw a 20 cm (8 in) square on the graph paper. Draw in the lines of your block, keeping all the proportions correct. Number each piece and show all the grain lines.

2 Draw the block again on the graph tracing paper, making sure all the templates are numbered and all the grain lines are shown. Carefully cut the individual templates from the tracing paper. It is important to keep the original drawing on the graph paper as you will need this for reference as you piece your block. The templates do not include a seam allowance. This must be added as you cut your pieces out.

CUTTING THE FABRICS

1 Lay the templates RIGHT SIDE UP on the RIGHT SIDE of the fabric, making sure the grain lines are correct. Pin them in place with flower pins which lie flat against the fabric, allowing your ruler to lie flat on the fabric.

2 Lay the ruler so that the 7.5 mm (¼ in) line is on the edge of the template and cut along the ruler's edge with the rotary cutter. Do the same for all sides of the template. You now have your fabric cut with a 7.5 mm (¼ in) seam allowance.

3 As you cut each template, add it to the block to ensure that you have cut it out

YOU WILL NEED

- 5 mm (¼ in) graph paper
- 5 mm (¼ in) graph tracing paper
- pencil
- flower pins
- fabrics
- rotary cutter and mat
- quilter's ruler

A graphed block

One template pinned on fabric

correctly, until you have laid out the entire block. Check the block against your master copy.

PIECING THE BLOCK

The shapes that you have created may be awkward shapes to work with, so you will need to work out a piecing order. You will also need to think carefully about the direction you will press seams. Butting the seams will help with the construction.

Also, you may need to slide pieces against each other so that the 7.5 mm (¼ in) seam allowance shows. Aim for smooth lines once your pieces are stitched and pressed. This may require some trial and error.

It is important to stitch an exact 7.5 mm (¼ in) seam allowance.

'One Yellow Triangle', 114 cm (45 in) square, machine-pieced, hand-quilted by CS, 1993.

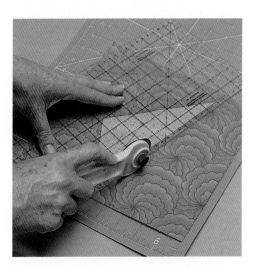

Cutting out the fabric using the template and the rotary cutter

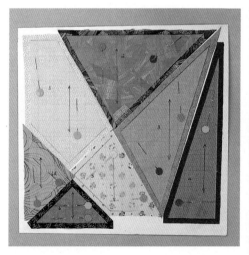

All the pieces cut out for the block

Floriade Pansies

I have enjoyed going to Canberra each September to see the wonderful flowers during Floriade. I have selected one of the drawings from page 41 and coloured it to fit my memories of those glorious flowers.

Machine-pieced, hand-quilted
Finished size of quilt: 139 cm (55 in) square
Finished size of block: 20 cm (8 in)
Finished size of embroidery: 11.5 cm (4½ in) square

CONSTRUCTING THE QUILT
See the templates on the Pull Out Pattern Sheet.

Making the templates
Note: There are thirty-six blocks, so you will need to cut thirty-six blocks of each template. Trace the templates onto the graph tracing paper. Number each one and show all the grain lines. Seam allowances are not included on the templates. Cut them out.

Cutting the fabric
Note: Although instructions are given for cutting out the whole quilt, it is preferable to cut out and make up one block first to be sure you have cut it correctly.

1 Place the template RIGHT SIDE UP on the RIGHT SIDE of the fabric, using flower pins. It is important to use these flat-headed pins so that your ruler will lie flat on the fabric. Use at least two pins for each one so that it does not move.
2 Lay your ruler with a 7.5 mm (¼ in) line against the edge of the fabric and cut along the ruler. Do this for all sides.
3 Cut the following pieces:
• 36 each of templates 1 and 5, using a variety of dark green fabrics. You could use one fabric for all of them, but a number of fabrics creates more interest
• 36 each of templates 4 and 8 in a variety of light green fabrics
• 36 of template 7 in a variety of light yellow fabrics
• 36 of template 6 in a variety of dark yellow fabrics
• 36 of template 2 in a variety of light pink fabrics
• 36 of template 3 in a variety of dark pink fabrics
• 36 of template 9 in a variety of purple fabrics
• 36 of template 10 in a variety of navy fabrics.

YOU WILL NEED
For the quilt
■ 5 mm (¼ in) graph tracing paper
■ rotary cutter and mat
■ quilter's ruler
■ flower pins
■ variety of fabrics. Use a number of purples, dark and light pinks, dark and light yellows, dark and light greens
■ small pieces of navy fabric for the pansy centres
■ thread to match
■ 3 m (3½ yd) of fabric for the backing
■ 150 cm (59 in) square of wadding
■ 40 cm (16 in) of fabric for the narrow border
■ 70 cm (28 in) of fabric for the wider border
■ 40 cm (16 in) of fabric for the binding
■ seed beads, size 10, in a golden yellow colour
For the embroidery
■ DMC Stranded Cotton, 2 skeins each: 552, 562, 743, 745, 955, 991, 993, 3607, 3609
■ DMC Stranded Cotton, 1 skein, 823
■ 20 cm (8 in) of Congress cloth
■ tapestry needle, no. 26
■ tapestry frame

Block layout

This lovely photograph inspired the quilt

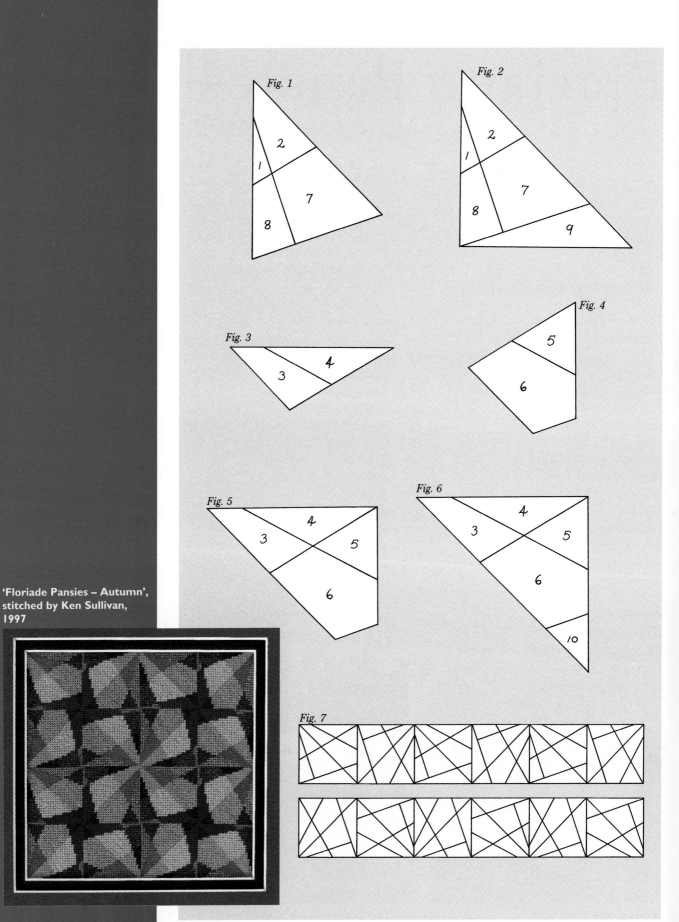

'Floriade Pansies – Autumn',
stitched by Ken Sullivan,
1997

'Floriade Pansies', machine-
pieced by CS, 1997, hand-quilted
and beaded by Norma Loch

Right: Detail of four blocks

Right: Detail of the beading

Right: Quilt layout

Making the blocks

Note: Sew the pieces together, using a 7.5 mm (¼ in) seam and matching thread.

1 Stitch pieces 1 and 2 together. Press the seam towards 1.
2 Stitch pieces 8 and 7 together, press the seam towards 7, then stitch this pair to the first pair, matching seams. Press the seam towards 1/2 (Fig. 1).
3 Stitch piece 1/2/7/8 to 9. Press the seam towards 9 (Fig. 2).
4 Stitch pieces 3 and 4 together. Press the seam towards 3 (Fig. 3).
5 Stitch pieces 5 and 6 together. Press the seam towards 5 (Fig. 4). Stitch this pair to 3/4, matching seams. Press the seam towards 5 and 6 (Fig. 5).
6 Stitch piece 10 to 3/4/5/6. Press the seam towards 6 (Fig. 6).
7 Join the two parts of the block together, matching seams. Make thirty-six blocks in the same way.

Assembling the quilt

1 Lay the blocks out in rows across the quilt, making sure the rotations are correct. Join the blocks into rows (Fig. 7). Press the seams of each row in the opposite direction to the previous row so that you can butt the seams as you join the rows.
2 Join the rows, making sure all the points and joins match.

For the borders

1 Measure across the centre of the quilt and cut two 5 cm (2 in) wide strips to this length. Pin them to the top and bottom of the quilt, matching centres. Stitch. Press the seam allowances towards the borders.
2 Cut two more 5 cm (2 in) wide strips the measured length plus 8.5 cm (3½ in). Pin them to the sides of the quilt, matching centres. Stitch. Press the seam allowances towards the borders.
3 Measure across the centre of the quilt and cut two 8 cm (3½ in) wide strips to this length. Pin them to the top and bottom of the quilt, matching centres.

Stitch. Press the seam allowances towards the borders.

4   Cut two more 8 cm (3½ in) wide strips the measured length plus 16.5 cm (7 in). Pin them to the sides of the quilt, matching centres. Stitch. Press the seam allowances towards the borders.

TO FINISH

1   Lay out the backing fabric (face down), the wadding and quilt top (face up). Pin or baste all the layers in place.

2   Finding interesting ways to quilt a rotated design is a challenge. I always try to keep the quilting simple so as not to detract from the design. For this quilt, I have quilted 7.5 mm (¼ in) inside the seam line of the deep purple areas, then again 7.5 mm (¼ in) inside that. In the pink, yellow and green areas, I quilted concentric shapes to fill the area. The border was quilted in a floral design, using a commercial template.

3   Add the bindings, following the general instructions for bindings on page 9.

4   Attach a label.

Beading

I thought it would look wonderful to have golden beaded centres for my pansies. Stitch on the beads, after the quilt is quilted and bound, using the fine needle. Work from the centre of each pansy in a fairly random way to create the lovely trailing golden centres. Stitch each bead through twice to make sure it stays in place.

'Floriade Pansies – Spring'
stitched by CS, 1997

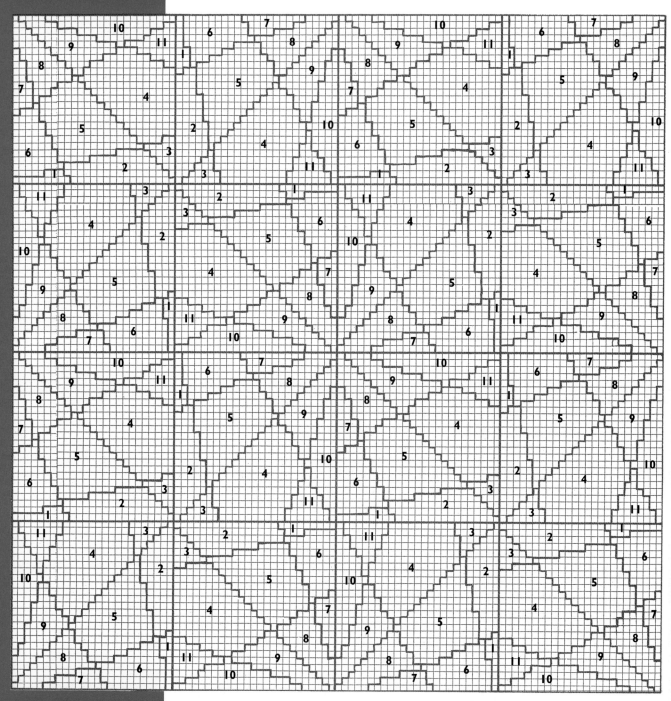

STITCHING THE EMBROIDERY

Using three strands of DMC Stranded
Cotton, complete the embroidery as charted.
See page 11 for stitching instructions.

KEY – DMC Stranded Cotton

	Autumn Tonings	Spring Tonings
1 –	223	552
2 –	815	552
3 –	902	823
4 –	3820	743
5 –	3822	745
6 –	469	993
7 –	936	991
8 –	722	3609
9 –	720	3607
10 –	471	955
11 –	730	562

Whirling

The play of colour in this pair was intended to be fun. Seeing the dynamic secondary design appear as I stitched the embroidery was quite thrilling. I just had to increase the size of the embroidery to see more of that exciting design.

Machine-pieced, hand-quilted
Finished size of quilt: 147 cm (58 in) square
Finished size of block: 20 cm (8 in)
Finished size of embroidery:
15 cm (6 in)
This quilt is made from design 3 on page 41.

CONSTRUCTING THE QUILT
See the templates on the Pull Out Pattern Sheet.

Making the templates
Note: There are thirty-six blocks, so you will need to cut thirty-six pieces off each template.

Trace the templates, making sure that each one is numbered correctly and all grain lines are shown. Seam allowances are not included on the templates. Cut out the templates carefully.

Cutting the Fabric
Note: Although the instructions are given here for cutting the whole quilt, it is better to cut and make up one block first to be sure that you have cut it out correctly.

1   Place the template RIGHT SIDE UP on the RIGHT SIDE of the fabric, using flower pins. It is important to use these flat-headed pins so that your ruler will lie flat on the fabric. Use at least two pins so that the template does not move. Lay your ruler on the template with the 7.5 mm (¼ in) line against the edge of the fabric and cut along the edge of the ruler with the rotary cutter. Do this for all sides of the template.

2   Cut the following pieces:

•   36 of template 1 in a variety of yellows. (One yellow alone fabric will work, but a variety of yellow fabrics will create more visual interest.)

•   36 of template 2 in a variety of light pink fabrics

•   36 of template 3 in a variety of cream fabrics

•   36 of template 4 in a variety of red fabrics

•   36 of template 5 in a variety of light

Block layout

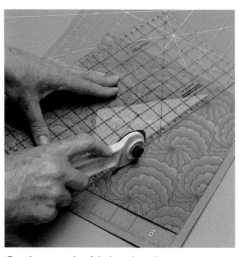

Cutting out the fabric using the template

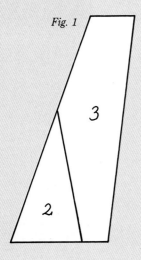

Fig. 1

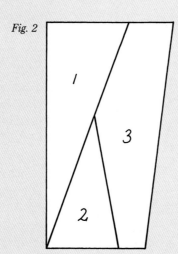

Fig. 2

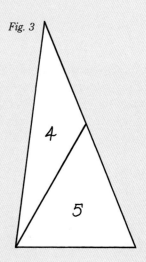

Fig. 3

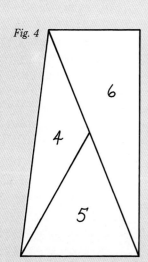

Fig. 4

Fig. 5

blue fabrics

- 36 of template 6 in a variety of teal fabrics.

Making the blocks

1 Lay out all the pieces for the block.
2 Machine the pieces together in the following order, using a 5 mm (¼ in) seam and a suitable thread.
- Stitch pieces 2 and 3 together, then press the seams towards 3 (Fig. 1).
- Add piece 1, then press the seam towards 1 (Fig. 2).
- Stitch pieces 4 and 5 together, then press the seam towards 5 (Fig. 3).
- Add piece 6, press the seam towards 6 (Fig. 4).
- Join the two parts of the block together. Press.
3 Make thirty-six blocks.

'Whirling', machine-pieced by CS, 1997;
hand-quilted by Norma Loch

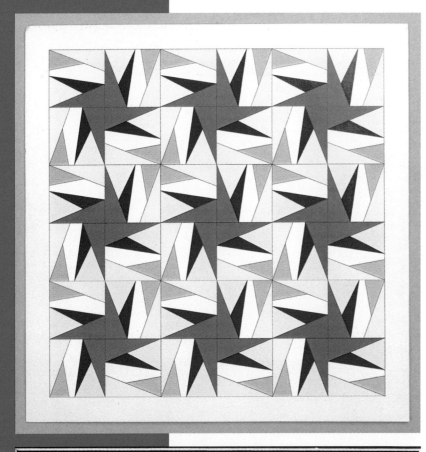

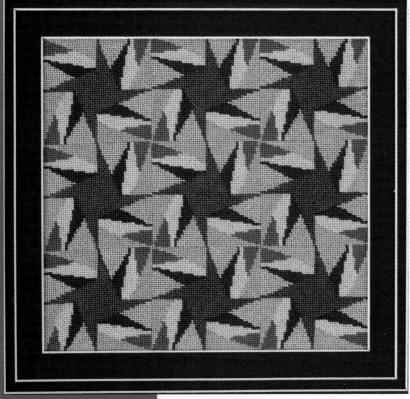

Assembling the quilt

1 Lay out the blocks in rows across the quilt, making sure the rotations are correct, then join the blocks (Fig. 5). Press the seams of each row in the opposite direction to the previous row, so that you can butt the seam as you join the rows.

2 Join the rows, making sure all joins and point match.

For the borders

1 Add the borders following the general instructions for borders on page 8. Cut the first narrow border 5 cm (2 in) wide, the second narrow border 3 cm (1½ in) wide a the wide border 10 cm (4 in) wide.

TO FINISH

1 Lay out the backing fabric (face down), the wadding and the quilt top (face up). Pin or baste all the layers in place.

2 This was fun to quilt. A simple scribbly patte was drawn onto the quilt, making sure that large area was left empty, then it was a sim matter of 'follow the line'.

3 Add the bindings following the general instructions on page 9.

4 Attach a label.

Top left: Quilt layout
Left: 'Whirling', stitched by
CS, 1997

150 x 150 stitches

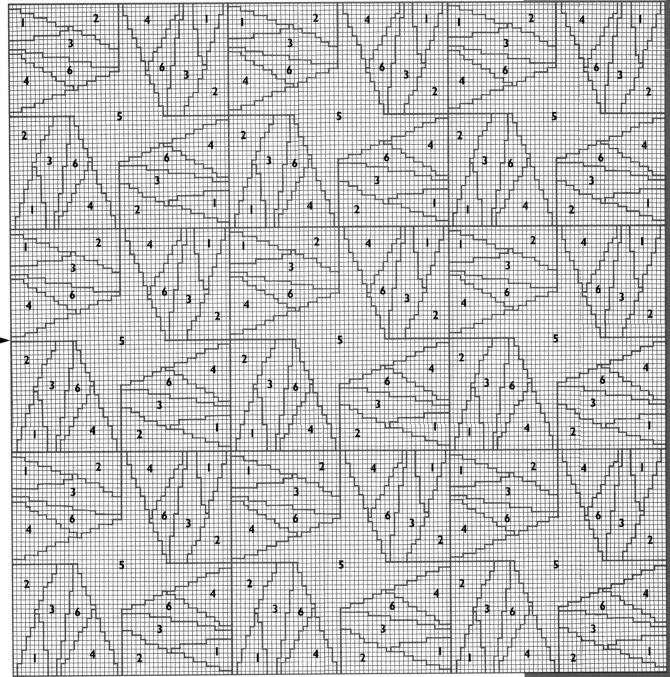

STITCHING THE EMBROIDERY

Using three strands of DMC Stranded Cotton, complete the embroidery as charted. See page 11 for stitching instructions.

KEY

DMC Stranded Cotton

1 – 3712
2 – 3822
3 – 3823
4 – 3811
5 – 3765
6 – 3803

Twisted Stars

YOU WILL NEED

For the quilt
- 5 mm (¼ in) graph tracing paper
- rotary cutter and mat
- quilter's ruler
- flower pins
- variety of print fabrics in dark purple, dark teal, black, light teal, yellow, mauve, and orange (reserve a special orange for the centre, if you wish)
- 75 cm (30 in) of fabric for the backing
- 75 cm (30 in) of wadding
- 30 cm (12 in) of fabric for the bindings
- thread to match

For the embroidery
- 20 cm (8 in) square of Congress cloth
- DMC Stranded Cotton, 2 skeins, 3799
- DMC Stranded Cotton, I skein each: 209, 211, 350, 550, 721, 726, 807, 3808, 3810, 3811
- tapestry needle, no. 26
- tapestry frame
- dark monofilament thread

The more I experiment with these rotated blocks, the more possibilities I see. Here, the centre squares of the design have been given a further turn to create their own rotation. Making a colour value change at the centre enhanced it further.

To do this with your own designs, draw the layout of your blocks, as described on page 39. Photocopy it, then cut out the centre four blocks. Cut them separately and reposition them with the rotation you wish at the centre.

Machine-pieced, machine-quilted
Finished size of quilt: 59 cm (23 in) square
Finished size of block: 15 cm (6 in) square
Finished size of embroidery: 11.5 cm (4½ in) square

This quilt is made from design 1 on page 41.

CONSTRUCTING THE QUILT
Note: There are sixteen blocks – four from light fabrics and twelve from dark fabrics. See the templates on the Pull Out Pattern Sheet.

Trace the templates onto the graph tracing paper. Number each one correctly and show all the grain lines. Seam allowances are not included on the templates. Carefully cut them out.

Cutting the fabric
Note: Although instructions are given for cutting out the whole quilt, it is preferable to cut and make up one block first to be sure that you have cut it out correctly.
1. Pin the template RIGHT SIDE UP on the RIGHT SIDE of the fabric, using flower pins. It is important to use these flat-headed pins so that the ruler will lie flat

on the fabric. Use at least two pins so that the template does not move. Lay your ruler with the 7.5 mm (¼ in) line against the edge of the fabric and cut along the edge of the ruler. Do this for all sides of the template (see page 44 for a picture of this step).
2. For the four light centre blocks, cut the following pieces:
- 4 each of templates 1 and 5 in light teal fabric
- 4 each of templates 3 and 6 in light yellow fabric
- 4 each of templates 2 and 6R in mauve fabric
- 4 of template 4 in the same bold orange print for the centre.
3. For the twelve dark blocks, cut the following pieces:
- 12 each of templates 1 and 5 in dark teal fabric
- 12 each of templates 3 and 6 in orange fabric
- 12 each of templates 2 and 6R in black fabric
- 12 of template 4 in purple fabric.

Block layout

'Twisted Stars', machine-pieced and machine-quilted by CS, 1996

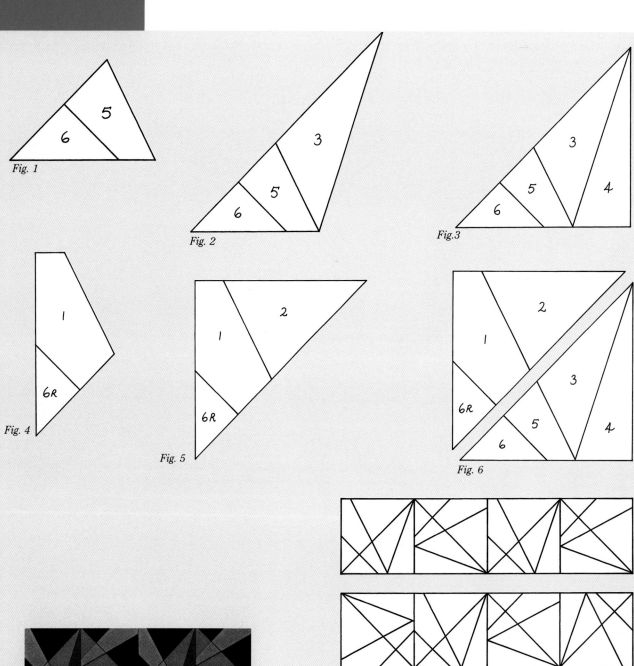

Fig. 1

Fig. 2

Fig.3

Fig. 4

Fig. 5

Fig. 6

Fig. 7

Quilt layout

Making the blocks

1 Lay out all the pieces for the block.
2 Machine-sew them together using a 7.5 mm (¼ in) seam and a suitable thread, in the following order:
* Stitch pieces 5 and 6 together, press the seam towards 6 (Fig. 1).
* Stitch piece 3 to 5/6, press the seam towards 5 (Fig. 2).
* Stitch piece 4 to 3/5/6, press the seam towards 4 (Fig. 3).

- Stitch pieces 6R and 1 together, press the seam towards 1 (Fig. 4).
- Stitch piece 2 to 6R/1, press the seam towards 2 (Fig. 5).
- Stitch these two large sections together along the diagonal edge, butting seams. Press the seam towards 6R/1/2 (Fig. 6).

3 Make sixteen blocks in the same way.

Assembling the quilt

1 Lay the blocks out in rows, making sure the rotations are correct. Stitch them together in rows (Fig. 7). Press the seams of each row in the opposite direction to the previous row so that you can butt the seams as you join the rows.

2 Join the rows, making sure all points and joins match.

TO FINISH

1 Lay out the backing fabric (face down), the wadding and the quilt top (face up). Pin or baste all the layers in place.

2 This quilt was quilted using a dark monofilament thread through the needle and a dark thread in the bobbin. Using a normal sewing stitch and the top tension slightly loosened, stitch 7.5 mm (¼ in) outside the shapes. You can combine shapes, if you wish. I treated all the teal areas as one shape.

3 Add the bindings, following the general instructions on page 9.

4 Attach a label.

'Twisted Stars, stitched by CS, 1997

and 8 from the right side of the tracing. Seam allowances are not included on these templates.

2 To cut the fabric, place the template RIGHT SIDE UP on the RIGHT SIDE of the fabric using flower pins. It is important to use these flat-headed pins so that your ruler will lie flat on the fabric. Use at least two pins so that the template does not move, even though these are very tiny pieces. Lay your ruler with the 7.5 mm (¼ in) against the edge of the fabric and cut along the ruler's edge. Do this for all sides of the template. Cut the following pieces:
- 36 of template 4 in a variety of medium pinks
- 36 of template 6 in a variety of dark reds
- 36 of template 7 in a variety of green-browns
- 36 of template 8 in a variety of light greens.

3 Stitch pieces 4 and 6 together (Fig. 1); press the seam towards 4. Set these thirty-six pieces aside.

4 Stitch pieces 7 and 8 together (Fig. 2); press the seam towards 8. Set these thirty-six pieces aside.

Working on the foundation
Note: For the rest of the fabrics you will need small pieces that will cover the area on the foundation. You only need approximate sizes as long as they fit. It is best to

overestimate the size, then trim the excess after stitching. You will be working with the traced side of the foundation towards you so you can stitch along the lines.

The step-by-step pictures show the right side of the foundation as the pieces are attached. Remember, you will be sewing on the WRONG side of the foundation.

1 Accurately pin piece 1 with its wrong side to the wrong (unmarked) side of the foundation (Step 1).

2 Lay piece 2 with its right side facing the right side of piece 1 along the seam line. Stitch along the traced line on your foundation, extending the stitching beyond the start and finish of the line. Trim away any excessive seam allowance. Push piece 2 back over the seam, finger-press and pin it in place (Step 2).

3 Stitch piece 3 on in the same way (Step 3).

4 Stitch piece 4/6 on in the same way, matching the seams accurately. You are trying to make a very straight line here so accuracy is essential (Step 4).

5 Stitch on piece 5 (Step 5).

6 Stitch on pieces 7/8, matching seams accurately (Step 6).

Assembling the quilt
1 Lay the blocks out in rows across the quilt, making sure the rotations are

Step 1

Step 2

correct (Fig. 3). Join the blocks into rows. Press the seams of each row in the opposite direction to the previous row so that you can butt your seams as you join the rows.

2 Join the rows, making sure all points and joins match.

For the borders

1 Cut four 2.5 cm (1 in) wide strips of medium-brown fabric, cutting from selvage to selvage.

2 Cut four 8 cm (3¼ in) wide strips of dark red fabric, from selvage to selvage.

3 Join each of the medium-brown strips to a dark red strip, using a 7.5 mm (¼ in) seam. Press the seams towards the dark red fabric.

4 Pin the centre of each border piece to the centre of the quilt side, then finish pinning the borders to the quilt. Stitch the borders in place, leaving 7.5 mm (¼ in) at the start and end of each stitching line. Do not worry about the excess fabric at this stage.

5 At each corner, with the right side of the quilt facing up, lay one of the corner extensions flat on your workspace. Lay the other corner across it, folded back at an angle of 45 degrees (Fig. 4). From the front of the quilt, match all the seams and pin, making sure you have a perfect point at the corner of the quilt. From the back, trim away excess fabric. Baste into place, then hem accurately from the front.

Step 3

Step 4

Step 5

Step 6

'Turquoise Flash',
foundation-pieced by
machine, machine-quilted
by CS, 1997

TO FINISH

1 Lay out the backing fabric (face down), the wadding and the quilt top (face up). Pin all the layers in place.

2 Machine-quilt, using monofilament thread through the needle and a polyester thread to match the backing in the bobbin. Using an ordinary stitch and with the top tension slightly loosened, 'draw' gently undulating curves from the top to the bottom. Always start at the centre of the quilt top and work out smoothly towards the edges.

3 Add the bindings, following the general instructions on page 9.

4 Attach a label.

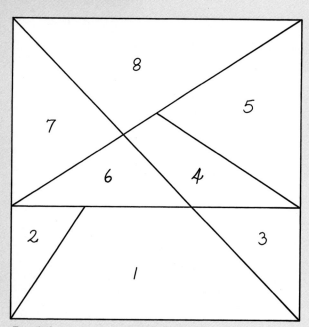

Foundation

KEY

1 Purple
2 Turquoise
3 Mauve
4 Medium Pink
5 Light Pink
6 Red
7 Green/brown
8 Light green

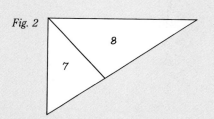

Fig. 1

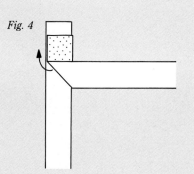

Fig. 2

Fig. 4

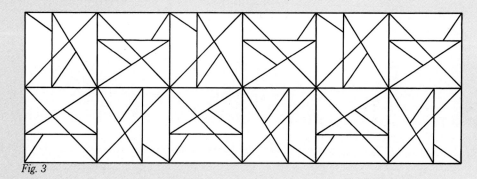

Fig. 3

'Turquoise Flash', stitched by CS, 1997

100 x 100 stitches

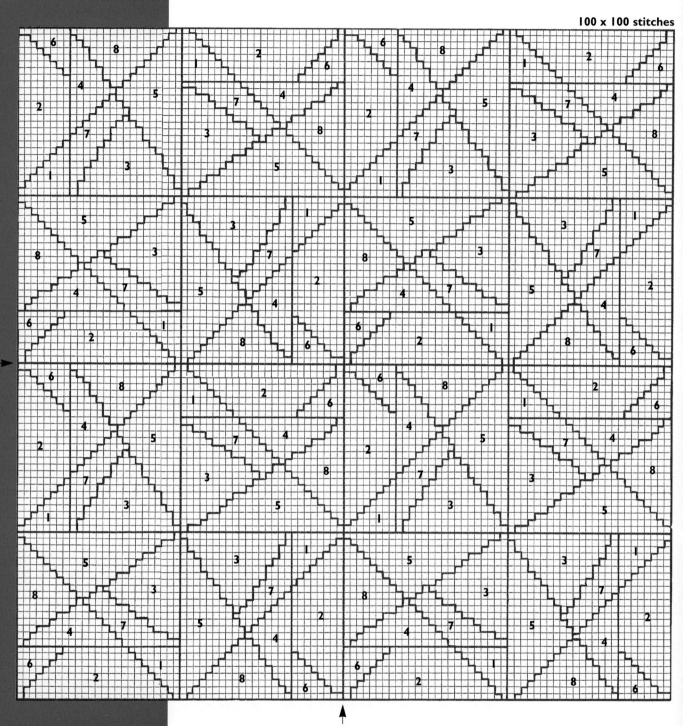

STITCHING THE EMBROIDERY
Using three strands of DMC Stranded Cotton, complete the embroidery as charted. See page 11 for stitching instructions.

KEY

DMC Stranded Cotton

1 – 211
2 – 327
3 – 778
4 – 816
5 – 928
6 – 996
7 – 3687
8 – 3790

Red Sails

Just to show how versatile and what fun creating your own designs can be, I have taken the block from 'Turquoise Flash' on page 61 and modified it to create a whole new look. Comparing the two blocks will show that I have started from a different point in the top right-hand corner and left out some lines, so that in fact the block itself has fewer pieces. Shading across the quilt has also changed the look. It is this colour change across the quilt which makes this quilt more challenging to make.

Foundation-pieced by machine, machine-quilted
Finished size of quilt: 63 cm (25 in) square
Finished size of block: 8 cm (3¼ in)
Total number of blocks: 36 (22 of Foundation A, 14 of Foundation B)
Finished size of embroidery: 10.5 cm (4¼ in)

This quilt uses design 4 on page 41.

CONSTRUCTING THE QUILT

See the foundations on page 72. There are two different foundations for this quilt: A and B. Although instructions are given for cutting the whole quilt, it is preferable to cut and make up one block first to be sure that you have cut out the pieces accurately.

Preparing foundations

With foundation-piecing you are always working from the back of the work. The foundations given on page 72 show how the blocks should look finished. Follow the instructions carefully for a successful quilt.

1   Trace the foundations onto the graph tracing paper as accurately as possible. Number each piece carefully.
2   Turn the tracings right side down and stick them to your desk or work surface. Using the felt pen, accurately trace over all the lines and number each piece on this reverse side.
3   You will need to cut an 11 cm (4½ in) square of Vilene for each block. Trace twenty-two of the reversed foundation A and fourteen of the reversed foundation B onto the Vilene squares. Make sure each foundation is numbered.

Cutting the templates

You will need to make some templates, as some of the pieces need to be joined before they are attached to the foundation.
1   Remove the tracings from the desk or work surface. Trace templates 5 and 6 from the right side of the tracing.
Note: Seam allowances are not included on these templates.

YOU WILL NEED
For the quilt
- light Vilene, no-iron
- 5 mm (¼ in) graph tracing paper
- fine black felt-tip pen
- rotary cutter and mat
- quilter's ruler
- flower pins
- masking tape
- a variety of small pieces of fabric for each colour: burgundy, bright red, gold and blue (Sort the blues into four values very dark, dark medium, light medium and light.)
- 20 cm (8 in) of yellow fabric for the inner border
- 50 cm (20 in) each of dark and light blue for the outer border
- 80 cm (32 in) square of fabric for the backing
- 80 cm (32 in) square of wadding
- thread to match

For the embroidery
- 20 cm (8 in) of Congress cloth
- DMC Stranded Cotton, 2 skeins each: 809, 798
- DMC Stranded Cotton, 1 skein each: 321, 800, 814, 820, 3820
- tapestry needle, no. 26
- tapestry frame
- monofilament thread

Quilt layout

2 To cut the fabric, pin the template RIGHT SIDE UP on the RIGHT SIDE of the fabric, using flower pins. It is important to use these flat-headed pins so that your ruler will lie flat on the fabric. Use at least two pins so that the template does not move, even though these are very tiny pieces. Lay your ruler 7.5 mm (¼ in) line against the edge of the fabric and cut along the ruler's edge. Do this for all sides of the template. Cut the following pieces:

- 36 of template 1 in a variety of red fabrics
- 36 of template 6 in a variety of burgundy fabrics.

3 Stitch pieces 5 and 6 together (Fig. 1). Press the seam towards 5. Set these thirty-six pieces aside.

Working on the foundation

For the rest of the pieces, you will need small pieces of fabric that will cover the area on the foundations. You need only have approximate sizes; it is best to overestimate the size and trim away any excess after stitching. You will be working with the traced side of the foundation towards you so that you can stitch along the traced lines.

Note: The steps for foundation-piecing are shown for 'Turquoise Flash' on page 56. The process for this quilt is the same although the pattern shapes are obviously different.

1 Accurately pin piece 1 with its wrong side facing the wrong (unmarked) side of the foundation.

2 For the fourteen foundation B blocks only, lay piece 7 with its right side facing the right side of piece 1, along the seam line. Stitch along the traced line on the foundation, extending the stitching beyond the start and finish of the line. Trim away any excessive seam allowance. Push piece 7 back over the seam, finger-press and pin it in place. At this stage, you will note that the correct placement of the various values of blue is very important. Refer to the Quilt Layout on page 69 to assist you.

3 Stitch piece 2 to all thirty-six blocks in the same way.

4 Stitch piece 3 to all thirty-six blocks in the same way.

5 Stitch piece 4 to all thirty-six blocks in the same way.

6 Stitch pieces 5/6 onto the foundation.

Assembling the quilt

1 Lay the blocks out in rows across the quilt, making sure the rotations are correct. Join the blocks into rows. Press the seams of each row in the opposite direction to the previous row so that you can butt the seams as you join the rows.

2 Join the rows, making sure all points and joins match.

For the borders

1 Cut four 2.5 cm (1 in) wide strips of yellow from selvage to selvage.

2 Cut two 8 cm (3¼ in) wide strips each of light blue and dark blue from selvage to selvage.

3 Sew a yellow strip to each of the light blue and dark blue strips, using a 7.5 mm (¼ in) seam. Press the seams towards the blue strips.

4 Pin the centre of each border piece to the centre of a quilt side, then finish

'Red Sails', foundation-pieced by machine, machine-quilted by CS, 1997

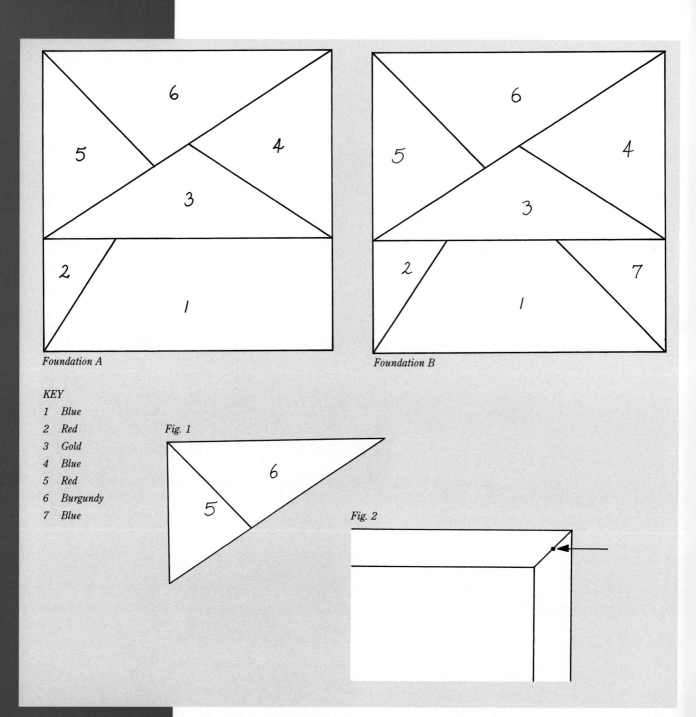

Foundation A

Foundation B

KEY
1   Blue
2   Red
3   Gold
4   Blue
5   Red
6   Burgundy
7   Blue

Fig. 1

Fig. 2

pinning the rest of the border in place. Stitch, leaving 7.5 mm (¼ in) at the start and end of each stitching line. Do not worry about the excess fabric at this stage.

5 At each corner, with the right side of the work facing up, lay one of the corner extensions flat on the work space. Lay the other corner across it, folded back at an angle of 45 degrees. From the front of the quilt, matching all the seams, pin the corner in place, making sure you have a perfect point at the corner of the quilt. From the back, trim away the excess fabric. Baste in place, then hem accurately from the front.

TO FINISH

1 Lay out the backing fabric (face down), the wadding and the quilt top (face up). Pin all the layers in place.

2 This quilt was machine-quilted, using a monofilament thread through the needle and a polyester thread to match the backing in the bobbin. Using an ordinary sewing stitch and with the top tension slightly loosened, 'draw' lines with the stitching, across the quilt.

3 Add the bindings, following the general instructions on page 9. Because I used two colours of binding to match the borders, the binding must start at one corner and this can make mitring the corner quite a challenge. I suggest that after you attach the binding, fold the fabric back at an angle of 45 degrees and stitch the two fabrics together to the halfway point on the front of the quilt (Fig. 2). Turn the binding to the back and poke the excess into the binding, then neaten off as best you can.

4 Attach a label.

'Red Sails', stitched by CS, 1997

Making the blocks

You will need to think about the gradations of colour as you make up the blocks. As each block has only three fabrics, I suggest that you make up a variety of blocks that include the following:

- all dark fabrics
- mostly dark fabrics with one medium
- mostly medium with one dark
- all medium
- mostly medium with one light
- mostly light with one medium
- all light.

The quantities of each that you make is up to you.

1 Stitch pieces 2 and 3 together, matching the straight edges (Fig. 1). Press the seam towards 2. Repeat for the other pair of pieces 2 and 3.

2 Stitch pieces 2/3 to either side of piece 1 (Fig. 2). Press the seam towards 2/3.

3 Add piece 4. Press the seam towards 4 (Fig. 3).

Assembling the quilt

1 Lay out all your blocks in rows on a sheet on the floor or a design wall, if you are lucky enough to have one. Aim for a nice gradation of colour across the quilt. You may need to change your mind a number of times, but this is all part of the fun!

2 Join the blocks together in rows across the quilt, making sure that you keep the colour layout correct (Fig. 4). Press the seams of each row in the opposite direction to the previous row so that you can butt the seams as you join rows.

3 Join the rows. Make sure all the joins and points match and that all the triangles point in the same direction.

For the borders

1 Cut the first border 6 cm (2¼ in) wide. Sew the borders to all sides.

2 Cut the second border 10 cm (4 in) wide. Sew the borders to all sides.

'Follow the Shades', machine-pieced by CS,
1997; hand-quilted by Cathie Bogard, 1997

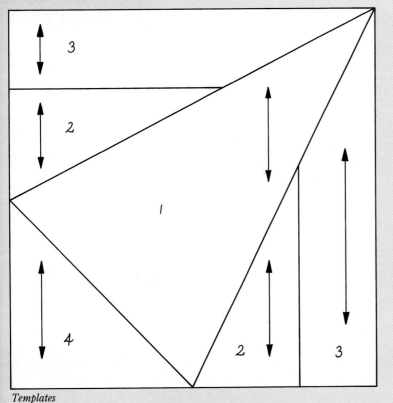

Templates

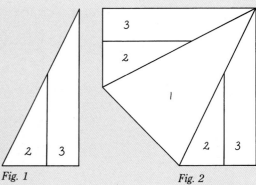

Fig. 1

Fig. 2

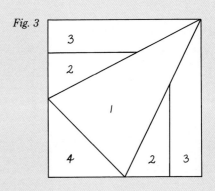

Fig. 3

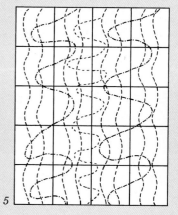

Fig. 4

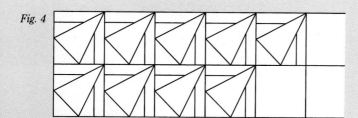

Fig. 5

3 For the last border, cut strips of fabric 4 cm (1³/₄ in) wide, from selvage to selvage, of at least eight fabrics, including the turquoise as it gives a good lift to the quilt. Stitch the strips together and press the seams in the same direction. Cut 7 cm (2³/₄ in) wide strips across this 'piece of fabric' you have made. Join these together to create strips that are the length of each side of the quilt. Attach the borders to the top and bottom of the quilt.

4 Cut 7 cm (2³/₄ in) squares for the corners and join them to the side borders, ensuring that the border length is the same as the quilt side.

TO FINISH

1 Lay out the backing fabric (face down), the wadding and the quilt top (face up). Pin or baste all the layers in place.

2 With all the joins in this quilt, the quilting had to be simple. It was quilted down the length of the quilt with gently undulating lines then, taking an undulating line with more movement, it was quilted again through the first lines, using the seam lines as a guide (Fig. 5). The striped border was quilted with straight lines through the centre of every second strip.

3 Add the bindings, following the general instructions for binding on page 9.

4 Attach a label.

STITCHING THE EMBROIDERY

Using three strands of DMC Stranded Cotton, complete the embroidery as charted. See page 11 for stitching instructions.

'Follow the Shades', stitched by CS, 1997

120 x 120 stitches

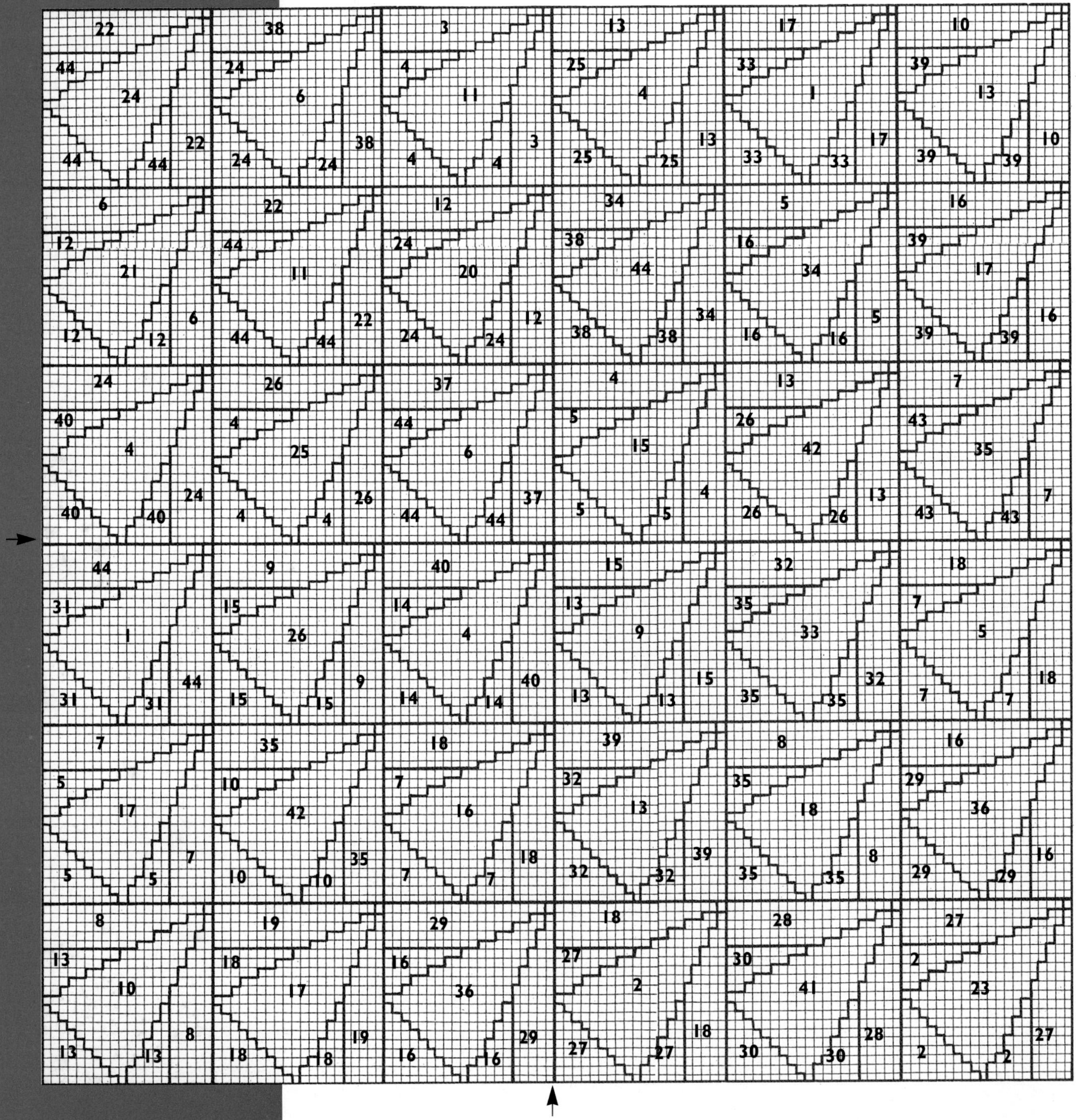

KEY – DMC Stranded Cotton

1 – 208	10 – 437	19 – 754	28 – 951	37 – 3722
2 – 211	11 – 550	20 – 807	29 – 3042	38 – 3731
3 – 221	12 – 552	21 – 814	30 – 3078	39 – 3733
4 – 304	13 – 554	22 – 815	31 – 3328	40 – 3746
5 – 316	14 – 603	23 – 818	32 – 3341	41 – 3756
6 – 333	15 – 721	24 – 823	33 – 3350	42 – 3766
7 – 340	16 – 722	25 – 902	34 – 3607	43 – 3778
8 – 341	17 – 742	26 – 917	35 – 3608	44 – 3803
9 – 350	18 – 744	27 – 948	36 – 3609	